AIRCRAFT OF THE ACES

136

ALLIED JET KILLERS OF WORLD WAR 2

SERIES EDITOR TONY HOLMES

136

AIRCRAFT OF THE ACES

Stephen Chapis and
Andrew Thomas

ALLIED JET KILLERS OF WORLD WAR 2

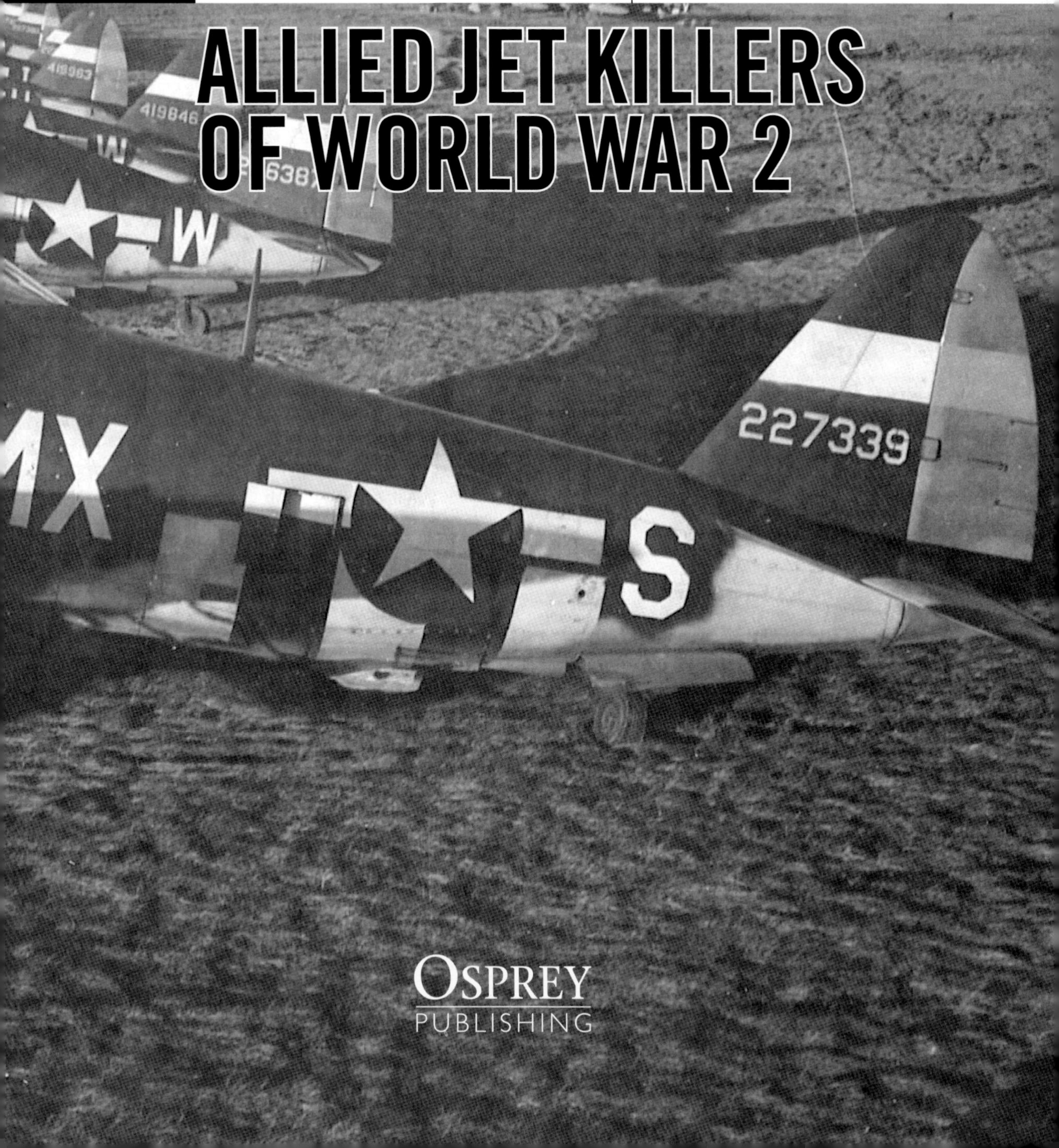

227339

OSPREY
PUBLISHING

Osprey Publishing
c/o Bloomsbury Publishing Plc
PO Box 883, Oxford, OX1 9PL, UK
Or
c/o Bloomsbury Publishing Inc.
1385 Broadway, 5th Floor, New York, NY 10018, USA
E-mail: info@ospreypublishing.com

www.ospreypublishing.com

OSPREY is a trademark of Osprey Publishing Ltd, a division of Bloomsbury
Publishing Plc.

First published in Great Britain in 2017

A CIP catalogue record for this book is available from the British Library

ISBN: PB: 978 1 4728 2352 6
          ePub: 978 1 4728 2353 3
          ePDF: 978 1 4728 2350 2
          XML: 978 1 4728 2351 9

17 18 19 20 21   10 9 8 7 6 5 4 3 2 1

Edited by Tony Holmes
Cover artwork by Mark Postlethwaite
Aircraft profiles by Jim Laurier
Index by Zoe Ross
Typeset in Adobe Garamond Pro, Helvetica Neue LT Pro and Trade Gothic LT Pro
Page layouts by PDQ Digital Media Solutions, Bungay, UK
Printed in China through World Print Ltd.

Osprey Publishing supports the Woodland Trust, the UK's leading woodland
conservation charity. Between 2014 and 2018 our donations are being spent on
their Centenary Woods project in the UK.

To find out more about our authors and books visit **www.ospreypublishing.com**.
Here you will find extracts, author interviews, details of forthcoming events and
the option to sign up for our newsletter.

Front Cover

On 25 March 1945 the 'Mighty Eighth' sent
its entire bomber force (although only 243
B-24s made it to their designated targets)
against oil refineries in Germany, and
amongst their powerful fighter escort were
Thunderbolts from the 56th FG. Maj George
E Bostwick, CO of the 63rd FS, was flying
P-47M 44-21160 *"Devastatin Deb"* when
his flight engaged a number of Me 262s
that were recovering at Parchim airfield.
Bostwick initially lined up behind one of the
fighters as its pilot made his final approach,
although he quickly shifted his sights to a
jet that was taking off. As Bostwick opened
fire his opponent banked sharply to the left
and the jet's wingtip dug into the ground,
causing it to cartwheel before exploding in
a fireball. This was Bostwick's sixth
success, and he claimed two more kills on
7 April to finish the war as an eight-victory
ace – he also had seven strafing kills to his
name. Squadronmate Capt John C
Fahringer scored his fourth, and final,
victory in 44-21160 when he shot down an
Me 262 on 5 April 1945 (*Cover artwork by
Mark Postlethwaite*)

Acknowledgements

The JG 400 archive photograph on page 30
was kindly supplied by Hans-Hermann
Cammann.

CONTENTS

CHAPTER ONE
AERIAL WARFARE REVOLUTION 6

CHAPTER TWO
FIRST CLASHES 17

CHAPTER THREE
BATTLES INTENSIFY 24

CHAPTER FOUR
BODENPLATTE TO *VARSITY* 45

CHAPTER FIVE
TO THE DEATH 62

CHAPTER SIX
ALL THE KING'S MEN 74

CHAPTER SEVEN
SOVIET VICTORIES 88

COLOUR PLATES COMMENTARY 91
INDEX 96

AERIAL WARFARE REVOLUTION

Contrary to popular belief, most of the jet- and rocket-powered aircraft developed by the Third Reich were not born out of desperation following the success of Operation *Overlord*. During World War 2, the Luftwaffe brought four jet- and rocket-powered aircraft into operational service – namely the Arado Ar 234, Heinkel He 162 and Messerschmitt Me 262 and Me 163. The initial design concepts for these aircraft, save the He 162, not only pre-date the US entry of into the war, but also the Battle of Britain!

Rocket-powered flight was pioneered in Germany. On 11 June 1928, Fritz Stamer made the world's first rocket-powered flight in a tailless glider fitted with a pair of black-powder rockets. It was called the *Ente* (Duck). The *Ente* was designed by Alexander Martin Lippisch, who was instrumental in the design and development of the world's only rocket-powered interceptor to be used in combat, the Me 163 Komet. During the course of World War 2 nine Komets were shot down in aerial combat by USAAF and RAF fighters, while in return, Me 163 pilots claimed 16 aerial victories – mostly B-17 Flying Fortresses and B-24 Liberators.

The radical and revolutionary Me 163 traces its roots all the way back to 1921 and the tailless delta-wing (flying wing) glider designed by Friedrich Wenk, founder of Weltensegler GmbH where Lippisch was employed. Between 1921 and 1926, while working at Weltensegler, Lippisch designed four tailless gliders designated Storch I to IV. In 1933, after a seven-

Veteran fighter pilot Hauptmann Otto Böhner, *Staffelkapitän* of 2./JG 400, prepares to take off from Venlo in Klemm-built Me 163B Wk-Nr 440014 in August 1944. This aeroplane was serving with the unit when I./JG 400 was declared operational with the Komet. Its final fate remains unknown (*EN Archive*)

year stint at the Wasserkupe-based Rohn Rositten Gedellschaft (RRG), Lippisch joined the glider research institute Deutscher Forschungsanstalt fur Segelflug (DFS) in Darmstadt-Griesheim.

By the time Lippisch went to DFS, his Storch design had matured into the Storch IX, which was followed by the Delta IV-series that began life as the Fieseler F 3 Wasp in 1932. On its very first flight, Gerhard Fieseler found the F 3 (with two 'push-pull' Pobjoy R radial engines) to be highly unstable and it subsequently crashed. After several design refinements and further crashes, Fieseler abandoned the aircraft, but Lippisch believed the problems could be overcome and acquired the rights to the F 3, which he re-designated the Delta IV. He duly refined the aircraft over successive variants, creating the Delta IVa, b and c. In 1936, the latter aeroplane, powered by a single 75 hp Pobjoy R radial engine, was sent to the Luftwaffe flight test centre in Rechlin, where it was put through its paces by Heinrich Dittmar. The aircraft, which was subsequently granted an airworthiness certificate and redesignated DFS 39, was the first of Lippisch's designs to resemble the Me 163. The following year the RLM issued a contract for Lippisch to build a second DFS 39 that would be powered by a 'special powerplant' – a liquid-fuel rocket built by Hellmuth Walter.

This second prototype was not a new aircraft, but a rebuild of the two-seat propeller-driven pusher aircraft, designated DFS 40, that Lippisch had built in 1937. On 2 January 1939, Lippisch and his team were transferred to the top-secret 'Department L' at Messerschmitt in Augsburg, where they modified the DFS 194 (renamed *Project X*) to accept the 660-lb thrust Walter HWK R-1-203, the same motor that powered the Heinkel He 176. After a delay brought on by the start of World War 2 in September 1939, engine trials began at Peenemünde, on Germany's Baltic Sea coast, in October and the DFS 194 itself arrived in February 1940. After a number of unpowered flights, Dittmar made the first powered flight on 3 June 1940, and soon the DFS 194 proved to be far superior to the He 176.

In early 1941, the *Reichsluftfahrtministerium* (RLM – Ministry of Aviation) ordered Messerschmitt to construct two prototypes that would carry the designations Me 163A V4 and V5. The former made its first unpowered flight from Lechfeld on 13 February 1941. Shortly thereafter, the same aircraft, towed aloft by a Bf 110, reached a speed of 531.25 mph in an unpowered dive. After being moved to Peenemünde the prototype made its first powered flight on 10 August 1941 and soon set a world speed record of 471.87 mph. Then, on 2 October, fitted with an HWK RII-203 motor, which used T-Stoff and Z-Stoff high-test peroxide propellants, Dittmar set an unofficial speed record of 627.29 mph (0.84 Mach) in a dive. He explained post-flight that he could have gone faster had he not encountered what would later become known as 'compressibility' (a change in the density of the air around an aeroplane at transonic speed as it approached Mach 1).

Shortly after Dittmar's historic flight, Ernst Udet, *Generalluftzeugmeister* (Luftwaffe Director-General of Aviation Equipment), ratified Messerschmitt's proposal to have Wolfgang Hirth Werke produce eight pre-production Me 163A-0 *Antons* and four production standard Me 163B *Berthas,* which were followed by a further 66 B-models built in the Regensburg-Obertraubling facility.

Due to difficulties experienced in mass-producing the improved HWK 109-509 rocket motor and near-constant design changes to the aircraft itself, the programme suffered continuous setbacks throughout 1942-43. Nonetheless, *Erprobungskommando* (EKdo) 16, a special flight test unit, was formed at Peenemünde on 20 April 1942 under the command of Major Wolfgang Späte. The purpose of EKdo 16 was to train pilots and mechanics and to develop maintenance procedures and combat tactics. Initially, the unit had only the V4 and V5 prototypes on strength, but by November 1942 there were a number of *Antons* and five *Berthas* available for training.

After the devastating RAF Bomber Command raid on Peenemünde on 17/18 August 1943, EKdo 16 operations were moved to Bad Zwischenahn, near Oldenburg, where flight testing continued with seven *Antons* and a single *Bertha*. The unit suffered its first fatalities in late 1943, with Josef Pöhs (a close friend of Späte) being one of those killed when, on 30 December, his engine failed on takeoff. Lacking sufficient altitude to bail out, Pöhs attempted a manoeuvre that pilots had been taught *not* to do – he tried to turn back towards the runway. Pöhs actually completed the turn, but when he rolled out there was a radio antenna directly in his flight path. Lacking the momentum to fly around the obstruction, he clipped the antenna with his left wingtip and the Me 163 cartwheeled into the ground.

Despite these setbacks, activity was picking up at Bad Zwischenahn by February 1944, when the first operational Me 163 unit, 20./JG 1, was formed and ten pilots began their training with the co-located EKdo 16, which consisted of nine operational *Berthas*. On 1 March 20./JG 1 was redesignated 1./JG 400 and transferred to Wittmundhafen under the command of Hauptmann Herbert Olejnik. The unit's first pilots began their training here, and by the end of the month six Me 163Bs had been delivered to Bad Zwischenahn.

On 14 May Späte made history when he gave the rocket-powered fighter its combat debut. Flying the Me 163B V41, which was fitted with the HWK 109-509A-2 motor that gave the *Bertha* a top speed of 596 mph, Späte's aircraft was painted bright red in honour of legendary World War 1 ace Manfred Freiherr von Richthofen. Fighter controllers on the ground directed Späte toward a group of USAAF fighters, and just as he spotted a pair of P-47 Thunderbolts above him, his engine quit. He managed to restart it after two minutes and set off after the American fighters, but as he reached 565 mph the Me 163 entered compressibility and flamed out again, thus allowing the P-47s to escape. Späte flew a second sortie later that same day, and endured similar problems.

The first production-standard Me 163B reached Wittmundhafen in mid-May 1944, and by early June 1./JG 400 had 16 fighters on strength. On 12 and 13 June demonstration flights took place for senior staff officers in the Jagdwaffe, Reichsmarschall Hermann Göring and Generalfeldmarschall Erhard Milch and delegations from Italy and Japan, which were both interested in the revolutionary interceptor. On 14 July, 1./JG 400 moved operations to Brandis, near Leipzig, and five days later

Major Wolfgang Späte, as CO of special flight test unit EKdo 16, made history on 14 May 1944 when he gave the rocket-powered Me 163B its combat debut. His attempt to attack a pair of P-47s was thwarted when he suffered intermittent problems with the HWK 109-509A-2 motor in his all-red Komet. Switching to the Me 262 in April 1945, Späte claimed five victories (all B-17s, which took his final tally to 99) whilst serving as the last *Kommandeur* of III./JG 7 *(EN Archive)*

Unteroffizier Kurt Schiebeler flew the first combat sortie at the controls of the Me 163B V50 – he made an unsuccessful attempt to intercept a P-38 Lightning. Then, finally, on 29 July 1944, the Komets of JG 400 clashed with USAAF fighters for the first time.

LOST TO HISTORY – He 280

While the Me 262 rightfully holds the title of the world's first *operational* jet fighter, it was not the first jet-powered fighter to fly. This historic bragging right goes to the nearly forgotten Heinkel He 280, which was inspired by Ernst Heinkel's emphasis on high-speed flight research and built on his company's experience with the He 178, the world's first jet-powered aircraft, which made its maiden flight on 27 August 1939.

Designed by Robert Lusser and initially designated He 180 in 1939, the fighter featured elliptical wings, twin vertical stabilisers fitted to a horizontal stabiliser with a slight amount of dihedral and designed from the outset with tricycle landing gear and a compressed-air ejection seat. The latter was also a first in aviation history. The first prototype, He 280 V1, was completed in the summer of 1940, but with development of the Heinkel HeS 8 turbojet engine running into difficulties, the first flight – which took place on 22 September 1940 – was a glide test with ballasted pods fitted in place of the motors. On 30 March 1941, Fritz Schäfer strapped into the second prototype, He 280 V2, and took the world's first jet fighter up for its maiden flight under its own power. Less than a week later, Schäfer demonstrated the He 280 for RLM chief Ernst Udet, who was not overly impressed with the aircraft.

Over the next two years, development of the He 280 was hampered by ongoing engine problems. In 1942, RLM ordered Heinkel to abandon the HeS 8 and HeS 30 engines and focus on the development of the more advanced, albeit problematic, HeS 011. However, with the latter

The nearly forgotten Heinkel He 280 was inspired by Ernst Heinkel's emphasis on high-speed flight research and built on his company's experience with the He 178, the world's first jet-powered aircraft. On 30 March 1941, Heinkel's Chief Test Pilot Fritz Schäfer (seen here in the cockpit) took this aeroplane – the second prototype He 280 V2, photographed at Rostock-Marienehe – aloft. This was an historic occasion, for it was the first flight made by a jet fighter under its own power (*EN Archive*)

not expected to be ready for flight for some considerable time, Heinkel considered fitting the He 280 with BMW 003 turbojets, but that engine was also beset with problems.

During the search for a suitable powerplant, Heinkel fitted the first prototype with eight Argus As 014 pulsejets – the same engine that powered the V1 'buzz bomb'. With Helmut Schenk at the controls, the aircraft was towed to altitude on 13 January 1942, but before the pulsejets could be ignited the airframe began to accumulate ice and the pilot was forced to eject from the stricken machine. The world's first ejection seat worked perfectly.

The second prototype was re-engined with Junkers Jumo 004s, but these were much larger and heavier than the Heinkel engines around which the He 280 had been designed. The first flight with these motors took place on 16 March 1943, and it soon became clear that the He 280's performance was inferior to the Me 262 when fitted with Jumo 004s. Therefore, on 27 March 1943, Erhard Milch ordered Heinkel to abandon the He 280 and concentrate on bomber development – a decision that greatly upset Ernst Heinkel.

WASTED POTENTIAL – Me 262

It was fortunate for the Allies that Hitler wasted precious time forcing the RLM to develop and deploy the Me 262 as a fighter-bomber rather than as an air superiority fighter as 'The General of Fighters' Generalleutnant Adolf Galland pleaded. Had the jet been used against RAF and USAAF bombers from the outset, it could have seriously challenged Allied air superiority over the Continent and potentially prolonged the war, increasing losses on both sides.

After a series of meetings with the RLM, Wilhelm 'Willy' Messerschmitt began work on an airframe that could be fitted with either gas turbine engines or rockets. Dubbed 'Projekt 1065', the design was presented to the *Technische Amt* (Technical Service) of the RLM in October 1938, where it was officially endorsed, thus allowing Messerschmitt to proceed with the development of the aircraft that would become the Me 262. The Me 262 V1, fitted with a single Junkers Jumo 210 piston engine, made its first flight on 18 April 1941. The third prototype made the first flight with jet power on 18 July 1942, with Fritz Wendel at the controls. Up until this point the RLM had shown little interest in the programme, but following Wendel's flight it ordered five prototypes and ten pre-production aircraft (V11 through V20), followed by a further 30 on 2 October 1942. However, unlike the first three prototypes, these new aircraft would feature tricycle landing gear.

An Me 262A-1a standard interceptor fitted with racks for bomb-dropping trials in late 1944. Leipheim-built Wk-Nr 110813 has been loaded with two 500 kg SC 500 bombs. The cable from a generator cart is plugged into the aircraft to charge its battery. This machine was used for training purposes by III./EJG 2 in 1944, and in 1945 it is believed to have been assigned to JG 7 (*EN Archive*)

JV 44's Me 262A-1a Wk-Nr 111745, seen parked in the unit's 'start area' at Munich-Riem in April 1945. It was flown variously by Unteroffizier Johann-Karl Müller, Unteroffizier Eduard Schallmoser and probably other pilots in the final weeks of fierce aerial combat experienced by JV 44 (*EN Archive*)

In March 1943 Messerschmitt delivered Me 262 V4 to Lechfeld, just south of Augsburg, where it was flight tested by Galland. Although he was unhappy with the range of the new fighter, Galland sent enthusiastic reports to Milch and Göring, and asked that all production of Luftwaffe fighters, except for the Fw 190, be halted so all efforts could be put into building the Me 262. Although Göring refused to halt production of piston-engined fighters, he did order the Me 262 into mass production in June 1943.

At this point the Me 262 was poised to challenge Allied air superiority over Europe, but the Führer had other plans. Rightfully convinced that the first few hours of an Allied invasion would be decisive, Hitler envisioned several hundred Me 262s pinning down enemy troops on the beaches and thus preventing the establishment and breakout from the beachhead. This would buy time for Panzer units to be moved to the front to push the Allies back into the sea.

On 2 November 1943, Göring and Milch flew to Augsburg to inform 'Willy' Messerschmitt of the Führer's idea, and to ask him if the new jet could be configured to carry bombs. Messerschmitt's response was in the affirmative, and within a few weeks the design was modified to carry either a single 1100-lb weapon or two 550-lb bombs. On 26 November prototypes V4 and V7 were presented to the Führer, who was pleased with what he saw. On 23 May 1944, Göring, Milch, Galland and Reichsminister Albert Speer (Minister of Armaments and War Production) met with Luftwaffe elite at Berchtesgaden. When the Führer was told that none of the production Me 262s that had been built to date had been modified to carry bombs, he launched into one of his furious tirades that ended with Göring making the bold statement, 'But my Führer, even a little child can see that it's a fighter not a bomber!' Hitler was unwavering in his conviction, so development of the Me 262 fighter-bomber proceeded. By this time test unit EKdo 262 had been formed at Lechfeld to introduce the jet into service and train the initial cadre of pilots.

The Allies had scant intelligence on the Me 262, but its very existence was cause for great concern. They knew if the Germans had a jet it was certain to be faster than any of their piston-engined fighters. The first hard evidence of the performance of the Me 262 came on 26 July 1944 when future five-victory jet ace Leutnant Alfred Schreiber of EKdo 262 damaged a Mosquito PR XVI photo-reconnaissance aircraft from No 540 Sqn, which made an emergency landing in Italy. On 8 August 1944, history was made when Leuteant Joachim Weber (again from EKdo 262) scored the first confirmed victory for a jet fighter when he downed a No 540 Sqn Mosquito PR XVI near Munich.

It has been impossible to determine exactly how many Me 262s were produced during the war, but the generally accepted number stands at just over 1400 examples, with approximately 1200 of these being delivered to 11 Luftwaffe test, fighter, bomber and reconnaissance units. By the end of hostilities, less than 200 aircraft were operational. Although the force was small, Me 262 pilots inflicted heavy casualties upon the Allies, claiming 542 aerial victories. The jet was flown by a number of aviators who had already achieved ace status in piston-engined fighters, and at least 28 *Jagdflieger* claimed five or more aerial victories in the Me 262, thus making them the world's first jet aces. The highest scoring jet ace of them all, nightfighter pilot Oberleutnant Kurt Welter, claimed 29 aerial victories (he was notorious for overclaiming, however).

After VE Day, a number of Me 262s were tested by American, British and French pilots, and in Czechoslovakia there were enough surplus parts available for Avia to produce nine single-seat S-92s and three two-seat CS-92s, which were test flown in 1947 and entered service in 1950 with the 5th Fighter Squadron. They were replaced by Soviet fighters in 1951, however.

BLITZ BOMBER – Ar 234

In 1940, the RLM authorised German aircraft companies to study the concept of a twin-engined jet reconnaissance aircraft with a range of 1325 miles. It would be powered by Junkers or BMW engines that were destined to be used in all three of the Luftwaffe's operational jet aircraft. In early 1941, Arado director Professor Walther Blume and company engineer Hans Rebeski put forth various designs, one of which was designated E 370 and later 8-324. The design was a high-wing monoplane powered by jet engines hung beneath the wings. It had an estimated range of 1250 miles, a top speed of 500 mph at 19,700 ft and a maximum ceiling of 33,000 ft. Originally designed around the BMW P 3302 engine, Arado modified the aircraft so it would accept either the Junkers Jumo 004 or Daimler-Benz ZTL 5 000 turbojet engines, although it was ultimately equipped with the former.

The aircraft was presented to the RLM in February 1942, and that April two prototypes were ordered and officially designated Ar 234. These first two, V1 and V2, were built rather quickly, but like every other German jet aircraft of this period, flight tests were delayed by a lack of engines. In this case the two Jumo 004B-0s were not delivered to Arado until February 1943 because Messerschmitt had priority on jet engine deliveries. The Ar 234 V1 was dismantled on 18 April 1943 and taken by road to Rheine, where the Jumos were installed in their nacelles. After a series of taxi tests, Flugkapitän Heinz Selle, Arado's chief pilot, took the V1 aloft for the first time on 30 July 1943. On its second flight that same day it reached a top speed of 406 mph. Selle was subsequently killed in the crash of the first production Ar 234A on 1 October 1943 after the left engine caught fire. This accident had no effect on the programme, and at around the same time the RLM ordered Arado to produce a bomber version of the jet, which led to the Ar 234B *Blitz* (Lightning), although pilots nicknamed the aircraft 'Hecht' (Pike). This variant was the first to be equipped with tricycle landing gear.

Throughout early 1944, production of the Blitz was hampered by Allied bombing, but when the Allies launched Operation *Overlord* on 6 June 1944 it presented an opportunity for the Ar 234 to prove its worth. German

The Ar 234 V1 prototype sits on its jettisonable three-wheeled take-off trolley (note that its central landing skid has also been extended) at Rheine airfield during the early stages of the aircraft flight test programme in the late summer of 1943. Arado's Chief Test Pilot Flugkapitän Heinz Selle performed the V1's first flight on 30 July 1943 (*EN Archive*)

high command did not know the exact strategic situation in Normandy. They needed reconnaissance flights to be undertaken over the beachhead, and the Ar 234 was the only aircraft that was capable of performing these hazardous missions and still making it back to base. The V5 and V7, both of which were equipped with RB 50/30 cameras, were duly passed on to a specially formed unit – the *Versuchsverband Oberkommando der Luftwaffe* (VV OKL) – at Oranienberg, where they were flown by Oberleutnant Horst Götz and Leutnant Erich Sommer. On 25 July 1944, Götz and Sommer were ordered to forward deploy to Juvincourt, near Reims in France, but only Sommer successfully completed the flight as Götz was forced to turn back with mechanical issues.

Although Sommer and the Ar 234 were ready to fly the world's first jet reconnaissance mission, he had to wait for more than a week for the takeoff dolly and other assorted launch equipment to reach Juvincourt. Finally, on 2 August 1944, everything was in place and Sommer took off and photographed Normandy and western France from almost 30,000 ft while flying at 440 mph. Sommer and the V5 were soon joined by Götz and the V7, and for the next three weeks the pair completed 13 missions between them over France and Great Britain. They flew these missions unopposed because the Allies were totally unaware of their presence.

By September 1944, VV OKL had been pushed back to Rheine, near Osnabruck in Germany, where the unit was eventually disbanded because production series aircraft, with conventional landing gear, were now available. A new unit, *Kommando 'Sperling'*, was organised with three pilots and three pre-production Ar 234B-0s, which had been replaced by nine production aircraft by 1 November. During the month the Allies finally became aware of this new aircraft when a flight of 339th Fighter Group (FG) P-51 Mustangs spotted a Blitz high over Holland and were unable to intercept the jet. It would not take long, however, for the first Ar 234 to fall to the guns of Allied fighters.

DESPERATE TIMES – He 162

By August 1944, just 120 Me 262s had been delivered to the Luftwaffe, and with American and British bombers pounding the Reich day and night, the Nazis searched for a way to produce more fighters to repel these raids. Thus, the idea of the *Volksjäger* (People's Fighter) was born. Developed by Karl Otto Saur, whom Albert Speer had put in charge of Luftwaffe re-equipment, and supported by Hermann Göring, the concept behind the *Volksjäger* was to design a simple jet fighter that was capable of outperforming Allied piston-engined rivals while being flown by basically trained pilots drawn from the Hitler Youth.

The diminutive size of the He 162A-1, together with its Lippisch-designed wingtips and slanting tail fins, are shown clearly in this view of what is believed to be JG 1's 'White 21' at Ludwigslust in April 1945. One member of the groundcrew is about to pull down the canopy, behind which can be seen a red and white engine intake cover which is marked with a '21'. The aircraft's nose has been finished in the national military colours of red, white and black, together with red arrows on either side. A generator cart is visible to the left of the photograph (*EN Archive*)

In desperation, the Emergency Fighter Programme was launched on 8 September 1944, with proposals submitted by Arado, Blohm & Voss, Fieseler, Focke-Wulf, Heinkel, Junkers and Messerschmitt for a fighter that could be designed quickly and built cheaply by semi-skilled or unskilled workers using non-strategic materials.

The fighter would be powered by the 1760-lb thrust BMW 003E engine and armed with a pair of MK 108 30 mm cannon. It was to have a top speed of 470 mph, a combat endurance of 30 minutes and be able to take off in less than 1700 ft while weighing 4000 lbs. The prototype would have to be ready by 1 December 1944, with production beginning a month later. 'Willy' Messerschmitt refused to participate in the programme, partly due to the unrealistic nature of the specifications and timetable, but mostly because he was busy developing the Me 262. By the middle of September the top two designs were the Heinkel P 1073 and the Blohm & Voss P 211, with the former ultimately being selected. On 28 September, the RLM placed an order for 1000 examples.

As if the programme was not fanatical enough already, at a conference held at the RLM on 17 October, it was decided that production of the new Heinkel fighter would begin on 1 November 1944 at a rate of 4000 aircraft per month – 1000 by Heinkel at Marienehe, 1000 by Junkers at Bernberg and 2000 by Mittelwerk GmbH in the hellish underground facility at Nordhausen.

Known within Heinkel as the Salamander or *Spatz* (Sparrow) and originally designated He 500, the new fighter would enter service as the He 162. First flown on 6 December 1944 by Heinkel test pilot Flugkapitän Gotthold Peter, the He 162 M1 (Wk-Nr 200001) demonstrated longitudinal instability due to the dorsal-mounted engine and tail surfaces that were too small. Regardless, Peter took the fighter up to an incredible 525 mph at 1900 ft. Four days later, he was killed when the M1 disintegrated during a high-speed pass (450+ mph) for high ranking officials. Despite Peter's death, the programme proceeded unhindered, and the second prototype, M2 Wk-Nr 200002, which was identical to M1, made its first flight on 22 December with Karl Francke at the controls. The next two aircraft, M3 and M4, were ready by 16 January 1945, and they differed from the first two prototypes through the introduction of a redesigned trailing edge, wingtips that were canted downward at 55 degrees, enlarged tail surfaces

Five pilots of 3./JG 1 relax at their dispersal in 1945. Second from right is Fahnenjunker-Feldwebel Günther Kirchner, who first flew the He 162 on 4 April 1945. He would be killed two weeks later when he attempted to eject from his Heinkel after being attacked by enemy fighters over Leck airfield. Also in this photograph, second from left, is Feldwebel Rolf Ackermann, who lost his life a few days after Kirchner when his He 162 crashed at Leck (*EN Archive*)

and ballast in the nose to shift the centre of gravity forward.

After a number of pre-production aircraft were built, quite rapidly, construction of the first production He 162A-1s and A-2s began on 20 January at the underground factory at Hinterbruhl. Once completed, they were rushed to the newly established test unit EKdo 162, which was also known as *Einsatzkommando* 'Bär' after high-scoring Luftwaffe ace Heinz Bär. By the end of January it had been decided that Fw 190-equipped JG 1 would be the lead operational *Spatz* unit. On 6 February 1945, a number of He 162s that had been built by Heinkel at Rostock-Marienehe were sent to Parchim and assigned to I./JG 1 under the command of Oberleutnant Emil Demuth. When the He 162s arrived, I. *Gruppe*'s Fw 190s were transferred to II./JG 1. Over the next ten days nearly 30 He 162s were issued to the unit, after which II. *Gruppe*, commanded by Hauptmann Paul Heinrich Dhäne, transferred to Vienna-Heidfeld to begin its conversion from the Fw 190 to the new jet fighter.

Over the next few weeks, before JG 1 was declared operational, a number of He 162s were lost due to pilots running out of fuel and either force landing or ejecting from their aircraft. These accidents made it glaringly apparent that Hitler Youth pilots would have been unable to fly the aeroplane, much less fight in it, after only a few hours of flight training. The He 162 quickly proved to be a very challenging aircraft to control when in the air, and a number of experienced Luftwaffe pilots were killed in accidents – post-war, a handful of British and French test pilots also perished while attempting to evaluate the jet fighter.

After having to move several times due to the rapidly approaching Red Army in the east and persistent USAAF daylight bombing raids in the west, both I. and II./JG 1 settled at Leck, on the northern coast of Germany. Here, I. *Gruppe* was declared operational on 15 April 1945. During the brief 21-day period that JG 1 was operational, 13 aircraft were destroyed and ten pilots killed. Most of these losses were again due to operational accidents. Indeed, available records show that only one jet was destroyed in combat. On 19 April Tempest V pilot Flg Off Geoff Walkington of No 222 Sqn claimed to have shot down an 'unknown type of plane with twin rudders and one engine' over Husum airfield. For many years there has been speculation that his victim may have been Fahnenjunker-Feldwebel Günther Kirchner of 3./JG 1.

While Kirchner was killed on this date, his demise was not as a result of Walkington opening fire on him. At 1222 hrs Leutnant Gerhard Stiemer and Kirchner took off from Leck, 20 miles north of Husum, to intercept enemy fighters spotted in the area. At the same time a pair of Tempests made a pass over the field. It was reported that Kirchner whipped his He 162 into a tight turn in order to pursue the RAF fighters – a fatal manoeuvre when at the controls of a *Spatz*. The fighter suddenly flipped over onto its back and began falling like a leaf. At that point Kirchner pulled the ejection handle, and, since the aircraft was nearly inverted, he was fired into the ground without his parachute ever opening. Seconds later one of the Tempests was shot down by a flak battery at Leck, its pilot bailing out and quickly being captured.

As previously noted, while this action was taking place over Leck, Flg Off Geoff Walkington was 20 miles to the south strafing Husum airfield. During a run across the field from south to north, he spotted an aircraft with twin rudders and one engine and gave chase as the unidentified machine rolled into a right turn. This manoeuvre allowed Walkington to close to within 1000 yards and open fire – he shot off two short and ineffective bursts. Walkington then followed his quarry up into the clouds, and at 3000 ft he passed the aircraft, which, he stated, was then spinning out of control. Walkington watched the aircraft continue to spin until it struck the ground and exploded near Husum airfield. Although his description of his alleged victim matches that of an He 162, only one *Spatz* was reported lost on that day and it was Kirchner's.

On 20 April RAF Typhoons were active in the Leck area and three He 162s were scrambled in what turned out to be an unsuccessful interception. A fourth *Spatz*, flown by Oberleutnant Wolfgang Wollenweber of 3./JG 1, did engage Typhoons that were again strafing Husum. While flying at more than 560 mph Wollenweber closed to within 100 yards of a Typhoon and pulled the trigger, but his MK 108 cannons remained silent. He overshot and lined up on a second Typhoon, buzzing the British pilot before zoom-climbing out of range.

Although it is difficult to determine precisely, it is generally accepted that He 162 pilots achieved two aerial victories. On 25 April Leutnant Hans Rechenbach of II./JG 1 claims to have shot down a British fighter, but there is no corresponding loss reported by the RAF. At 1138 hrs on 4 May, with Nazi Germany's surrender imminent, Leutnant Rudolf Schmitt of I./JG 1 took off from Leck in He 162A-2 'White 1' (Wk-Nr 120013) to engage Typhoons and Tempests roaming in the Husum area. Just seven minutes later Schmitt encountered one of the British fighters southeast of Husum and fired what appeared to be several effective bursts. Schmitt felt that he had damaged the fighter enough that it went down. Leutnant Schmitt's apparent aerial victory occurred on what was likely the last combat sortie flown by JG 1.

Later that day I. and II./JG 1 were merged and placed under the command of Oberstleutnant Herbert Ihlefeld, who arranged to turn the remaining 22 He 162s, which were neatly lined up in rows on either side of one of Leck's taxiways, over to Allied intelligence. On 5 May 1945, Generaladmiral Hans-Georg von Freideburg ordered German forces in northwest Europe to surrender. The next day elements of the British 11th Armoured Division reached Leck and accepted the surrender of the Luftwaffe's sole He 162 unit.

Shortly after the German surrender in early May 1945, JG 1 organised its He 162s into two neat rows on Leck airfield in anticipation of the arrival of British air intelligence specialists who were eager to learn more about German jet aircraft technology. The jet closest to the camera is He 162A-1 Wk-Nr 120067 'White 4' of 1./JG 1 (*EN Archive*)

CHAPTER TWO

FIRST CLASHES

Prior to joining the 78th FG in August 1944 to take command of the 82nd FS, Maj Joseph Myers had scored three victories flying P-38s with the 55th FG. Following his shared Me 262 kill with 2Lt Croy on 28 August 1944, Myers claimed his final victory on 7 October 1944, thus finishing the war just a half-kill short of 'making ace'. Maj Myers was flying P-47D-27 42-27339 when he shot down the 1./KG 51 Me 262 flown by Oberfeldwebel Hieronymous Lauer on 28 August 1944 (*USAAF*)

The renowned Eighth Air Force historian Roger Freeman coined a simple phrase to describe the Luftwaffe's revolutionary new aircraft – the jet menace. Allied intelligence had been aware of Germany's jet programmes for several months, and heavy bombers soon began targeted attacks on suspected manufacturing plants and airfields. The first actual sighting, however, did not occur until 28 July 1944.

That day, Mustangs of the 359th FG were escorting 45th Bomb Wing (BW) B-17s that had been sent to attack oil industry targets near Merseburg and Leuna, in eastern Germany. At the same time several Me 163s from I./JG 400 were airborne on training flights, and two of the pilots made feigned attacks on the Flying Fortresses. These passes resulted in a brief, inconclusive, engagement with several 359th P-51s, including the aeroplane flown by group CO, Col Avelin Tacon, who later reported;

'My eight-ship section was furnishing close support to a combat wing of B-17s that had just bombed Merseburg. The bombers were heading south at 24,000 ft and we were flying parallel to them about 1000 yards to the east at 25,000 ft. Someone called out "contrails high at six o'clock". I looked back and saw two contrails at about 32,000 ft about five miles away. I immediately called them to my flight as jet-propelled aircraft. There is no mistaking their contrails. It was white and very dense – as dense as cumulus clouds and the same appearance, except it was elongated. The two contrails I saw were about three-quarters of a mile long.

'We immediately dropped tanks and turned on gun switches while making a 180-degree turn back towards the bandits. It has since turned out in interrogation that there were five Me 163s – one flight of two, which I saw with jets on, and another flight of three without jets. The two I saw made a diving turn to the left, in good close formation, and started a "six o'clock" pass on the bombers. As soon as they turned they cut off their jets. We started a head-on overhead pass at them, getting between them and the rear of the bombers. When they were still about 3000 yards from the bombers they saw us and made a slight turn to the left into us, and away from the bombers. Their bank was about 80 degrees in this turn, but they only changed course 20 degrees. They did not attack the bombers. Their roll rate appeared to be excellent, but radius of the turn very large. I estimate, conservatively, they were doing between 500-600 mph.

'Although I had seen them start their dive and watched them throughout their attack, I had no time to get my sights anywhere near them. Both ships, still in close formation and without jet propulsion, passed about 1000 ft under us. I split-essed to try to follow them. As soon as they passed under us one of them continued on in a 45 degree dive and the other pulled up into the sun, which was about 50 to 60 degrees above the horizon. I glanced quickly up into the sun but could not see this one. When I looked back at the one that had continued the dive, approximately one second later, he was about five miles away down to about 10,000 ft. Although I did not see it, the leader of my second flight reports the aircraft that pulled up into the sun used his jet in short bursts. The flight leader described it as looking like he was blowing smoke rings. This ship disappeared and we don't know where it went.'

The Komets of I./JG 400 were airborne again the next day, and this time they tangled with P-38 Lightnings of the 479th FG, which was providing withdrawal support for a group of B-17s. Leading 'Newcross Yellow' Flight was future 14-victory ace Capt Arthur F Jeffrey, who joined the 479th FG's 434th FS in October 1943. It was a very cloudy day over Holland and Jeffrey noticed a straggler just above the undercast that was steadily falling behind the formation. The aircraft in question was B-17G 42-107997 *She Hasta* from the 100th BG, which had been severely damaged and had several wounded crewmen on board. Jeffrey, noticing the bomber was heading northwest – a heading that would cause it to miss England completely – left 'Yellow Three' and 'Four' at altitude while he took his wingman down to give *She Hasta* some close support and navigational assistance. Even though their P-38s looked like no other fighter in the world, the gunners of the rookie crew manning the Flying Fortress fired at the Lightnings as they approached. A short while later Jeffrey found himself engaging an Me 163, as he described in his Encounter Report;

'The B-17 plodded along at 11,000 ft, dodging holes in the overcast to keep out of the flak, and at 1145 hrs I observed an Me 163 in attack position behind it. The Me 163 made a slight low-side "five o'clock" pass at the B-17, followed through in a slight dive and then levelled off. At about this time the German must have seen me because he made another slight dive. He then started a very steep climb, weaving all the while, as though he was trying to see behind him. During this weaving I closed with him and opened fire, observing strikes on the Me 163.

USAAF fighters attempted to engage Luftwaffe jets for the first time on 28 July 1944 when Mustangs from the 359th FG tangled with Me 163s from JG 400 near Merseburg. The next day the P-38-equipped 479th FG was in the process of providing withdrawal support for a group of B-17s over Holland when Capt Arthur Jeffrey of the 434th FS/479th FG spotted a Me 163 preparing to attack a lost and struggling B-17G. Engaging the Komet, he scored numerous hits before following the Me 163 into a vertical dive in his P-38J-15 42-104425 *BOOMERANG* (seen here with a member of Jeffrey's groundcrew), which entered compressibility at 500 mph. Jeffrey pulled out just above the ground, but his wingman last saw the Komet enter the clouds at 3000 ft, still in a near vertical dive. This was Jeffrey's second aerial victory, and the only jet success credited to the P-38. Jeffrey would score two more victories in the Lightning and go on to become a double ace in the P-51 (*Peter Randall collection*)

'At 15,000 ft the pilot levelled off and started to circle to the left, as though positioning himself to attack me. I could turn tighter than he could, and I got a good deflection shot, with the closest range estimated to be 200 to 300 yards. I thought I was getting hits but my shots seemed too far away for effect when puffs of smoke started to emanate from the tail of the jet.'

Jeffrey seemed to think that the Komet pilot had never been in combat before, for it seemed like he did not know what to do. There are no records to indicate who the aviator was or what kind of combat experience he had, but he did do what most fighter pilots do instinctively – he turned into his attacker.

'At about 15,000 ft he turned and attacked, with me looking right down his throat', Jeffrey continued. 'We got into a tight circle and I saw some good deflection shots hitting him. Then he rolled over and went straight down, with me fire-walled behind him. For the first time in my life I found out how – at more than 500 mph – your props can act as brakes. I was shooting at him as I was going straight down, and my tracer path was walking forward of the "bat" [Me 163]. Then I got into an arc of an outside loop, and when I finally pulled out a few hundred feet above the ground, I blacked out'.

Jeffrey, flying P-38J-15 42-104425 *BOOMERANG*, quickly regained his senses, but by then the rocket fighter had vanished. He duly claimed it as a probable. While Jeffrey had been wrestling his Lightning out of the death-grip of compressibility, his wingman, 1Lt Richard G Simpson, watched the Me 163 enter the clouds;

'I started to pull out at 3500-4000 ft, indicating a little over 400 mph. The Me 163 went into the clouds, which were around at 3000 ft, still in a dive of 80 degrees or better. He must have been indicating 550-600 mph, and showed no signs of pulling out. I don't see how the German could have gotten out of that dive.'

To this day no records have been located that indicate the loss of an Me 163 on this day, yet Capt Arthur Jeffrey's probable claim was upgraded to destroyed, thus giving him the distinction of being the first Allied pilot to down a German jet. His Me 163 also proved to be the only jet/rocket-powered aircraft victory credited to the P-38. The second of four kills credited to Capt Jeffrey in the Lightning, he would go on score ten more victories in the Mustang and finish the war as the 479th FG's leading ace.

On 16 August 425 B-17s from the Eighth Air Force's 1st Air Division targeted oil refineries and aircraft plants in Delitzsch, Halle, Böhlen and Schkeuditz. Only three of these targets were within range of the Komets operating from Brandis, whose pilots would have to penetrate the defensive cover provided by 48 Thunderbolts and 241 Mustangs before they could engage the bombers. Unperturbed, the *Jagdflieger* from 1./JG 400 attacked five Flying Fortresses, including B-17G 42-31636 *OUTHOUSE MOUSE* of the 91st BG and B-17G 43-38085 *Towering Titan* of the 305th BG. The tail gunner aboard the latter aircraft, SSgt Howard Kaysen, managed to hit an Me 163 that had closed to within 50 yards. The Komet began trailing smoke and its pilot, Feldwebel Herbert Straznicky, who had been wounded by Kaysen's defensive fire, bailed out.

1Lt Reese Walker Mullins' *Outhouse Mouse* had already been damaged by Fw 190s from IV.(*Sturm*)/JG 3 by the time it was targeted by an Me 163, the B-17 proving to be an inviting target as it lagged behind the main bomber formation. Five-victory ace Leutnant Hartmut Ryll wasted little time in getting directly behind the aircraft and making a gliding attack on it at 1045 hrs, although he was unable to score any hits due to Mullins' aggressive evasive action. This attack had in turn been observed by a flight of P-51Ds from the 359th FG, led by 370th FS CO, and ace, Lt Col John B Murphy, who recounted the ensuing engagement in his Encounter Report;

'I was escorting our bombers southeast of Leipzig at 27,000 ft when I noticed a contrail climbing rapidly up towards the bombers from behind and to the port side. I recognised the contrail as being produced by a jet-propelled aircraft because of its speed. Due to its speed and altitude advantage, I knew I could not overtake him, but noticed a straggling B-17 to starboard at 25,000 ft which was headed north and east of Leipzig all alone, and I headed toward him, thinking that he probably would

Maj John B Murphy took command of the 370th FS/359th FG in early 1943, and he was the only pilot in the new group to have combat experience. He had fought the Japanese in the Aleutians, where he helped down an E8N 'Dave' floatplane whilst flying a P-40E. By 16 August 1944 now-Lt Col Murphy had 5.75 kills to his credit when he came to the aid of the crippled B-17G 42-31636 *OUTHOUSE MOUSE* of the 91st BG that was under attack by Me 163s. After damaging one Komet, Murphy attacked a second that attempted to escape by diving for the deck. He scored several hits that caused heavy damage, and the Me 163 was last seen in a dive shedding parts. Murphy was credited with one Komet destroyed and one damaged, finishing the war with 6.75 victories (*359th FG Association*)

On 16 August 1944, 2Lt Cyril W Jones was Lt Col Murphy's wingman, and after his flight leader attacked and overshot the first Komet, Jones moved in for the kill as the German split-essed into a dive. After getting a few hits on Me 163's tail, Jones increased his lead and fired a burst that shattered the canopy on the Komet and probably killed the pilot, Leutnant Hartmut Ryll, who became the first pilot from JG 400 to be killed in action. This was Jones' second victory. He 'made ace' on 11 September 1944 when he shot down four Bf 109s. The next day, on just his 16th combat mission, Jones was shot down by flak and killed while strafing an airfield south of Meiningen (*359th FG Association*)

be attacked. The jettie [sic] contrail ceased about 500 yards from the bomber, and from that point on I kept him in sight as I would any other aircraft. He passed through the bombers and went down to the straggling B-17, arriving there before I could. I wasn't far behind, however, and was overtaking.

'After he passed the B-17, he seemed to level off, and as I closed on him, I opened fire from about 1000 ft and held it until I overshot. I scored a few hits on the left side of the fuselage. I pulled up to the left as sharply as I could to prevent overshooting and getting in front of him, and lost sight of both him and my wingman. My wingman, Lt Jones, reported that the jettie flipped over on his back in a half roll, and as he did so, he scored a sufficient number of hits in the canopy to destroy him. As Jones tried to follow him through the dive, he blacked out.

'When I completed my sharp chandelle turn to the left, I saw another jettie off to my left and Jones farther off and lower to my right. I started down on this one, which was making rather shallow diving turns to the left. I think I must have followed him through two turns before overtaking him. I realised that I was going to overtake him rapidly too, but I did not fire until at a distance of around 750 ft, when I held a continuous burst, seeing a series of strikes the full length of the fuselage. Parts began falling off, followed by a big explosion and more parts falling off. I could smell strange chemical fumes in my cockpit as I followed through the smoke of the explosion. It seemed to me that a large chunk of the fuselage from the canopy on back just popped off with the explosion.

'I followed him part of the way down, and my intention was to follow him down until he hit [the ground], but I saw another jettie at my same altitude about two miles off and decided against it. Being by myself and low on gas, I did not attack the other jet, but headed home.'

Murphy claimed one Me 163 shot down and one damaged in the air. His wingman, future six-victory ace 2Lt Cyril Jones, who had scored his first aerial victory one week earlier, also filed a report following this engagement;

'I was flying "White Two" when "White Leader" called in a jettie making a pass at the bombers we were escorting. "White Leader" said to keep an eye on the enemy aircraft. We were about two miles from the bomber formation, and the jet aircraft was on the other side of the bombers. "White Leader" started a turn toward one bomber straggler which looked as if it might be a target for the jet aircraft – as we started the turn, I noticed three contrails similar to the one "White Leader" had called in. They were going through another formation of bombers. I could see no aircraft at the end of the contrails, but decided they must be other jet aircraft. I did not try to watch them longer and concentrated on following my leader.

'The enemy pilot that was trying to intercept completed his run on the formation of bombers, passing through them and heading for the straggler. He completed the run on the straggler and he passed about 500 yards in

front and to the starboard side of the bomber when we overtook him. "White Leader" was about 1000 ft ahead of me and about 500 ft above me on the final approach. I saw "White Leader" fire, and strikes appeared on the tail of the enemy aircraft. "White Leader" broke away and I continued in, the jet aircraft split-essed, and I followed him. I fired a short burst with a three-radii lead and observed no hits. I increased the lead and fired again. The entire canopy seemed to dissolve on the enemy aircraft, which I had identified as an Me 163. I closed very fast and broke behind him.

'As I passed behind the enemy aircraft, I hit his wash and did a half turn. While recovering, I blacked out and lost sight of the Me 163. I recovered at 14,000 ft after starting the attack at 23,000 ft. The pilot was surely killed when the bullets entered his canopy, and I claim one Me 163 destroyed.'

Jones's victim, Leutnant Ryll, became the first JG 400 pilot to be killed in action when his Me 163 crashed vertically southeast of Leipzig. He was subsequently credited with downing a B-17 prior to this death, taking his final tally to six. Feldwebel Herbert Straznicky and Feldwebel Siegfried Schübert were also awarded single victories over Flying Fortresses on this date.

A nearly forgotten footnote to the story of this oft-told engagement is that 1Lt Jimmy C Shoffit from the 370th FS broke into a Me 163 that was attacking a B-17, scoring hits on its right wing before the Komet escaped in a power dive. This was the closest Shoffit would get to claiming a victory prior to finishing his tour in April 1945. John Murphy's Komet kill took his final score to 6.75, as he finished his tour just two weeks later. Finally, 'Cy' Jones 'made ace' on 11 September when he shot down four Bf 109s in a single dogfight. Sadly, the very next day, whilst on only his 16th combat

A group photograph of pilots from the 370th FS includes two Komet 'killers', 2Lt Cyril W Jones standing third from the left and Lt Col John B Murphy standing on the far right. The 359th FG was credited with the destruction of six Luftwaffe jets during the war, the 368th FS downing a single Me 262, the 369th a pair of Me 262s and the 370th FS three Me 163s, making it the highest scoring USAAF squadron against the Komet (*Peter Randall collection*)

Although he never attained ace status, 2Lt Manfred O Croy made USAAF history on 28 August 1944 when he and his flight leader, Maj Joseph Myers, were credited with the downing of the first Me 262 by Allied fighter pilots. It was also Croy's first victory, and he later shot down a pair of Bf 109s on 26 November 1944. He was killed on 16 April 1945 while strafing Straubing airfield. Croy's body was interred in the Lorraine American Cemetery in St Avold, France (*Curtis Shepard*)

mission, Jones was shot down by flak and killed while strafing an airfield south of Meiningen.

Twelve days after the first Me 163 had been shot down, the Duxford-based 78th FG was tasked with strafing rail targets in Charleroi, Belgium. 82nd FS CO Maj Joseph Myers was leading 'Surtax Blue' Flight on this mission, having only recently taken command of the unit (he had previously completed a tour in the ETO with the 38th FS/55th FG) after Capt Charles Clark was shot down and captured on 2 August 1944.

'Surtax Blue' Flight was providing top cover while a number of other Thunderbolts went down to the deck. On this mission Maj Myers was flying his assigned P-47D 42-27339, with future jet killer 2Lt Wayne Coleman on his wing. The second element was led by 1Lt Fred Bolgert, with 2Lt Manfred Croy in P-47D 42-75551 on his wing. While flying at 11,000 ft near Brussels, Myers caught a glimpse of what he thought was a B-26 Marauder flying at low level and went down to investigate. When Myers got down to around 5000 ft he was indicating 450 mph and the unidentified aircraft began evasive action that allowed him to close to within 2000 ft above and astern. Myers later noted in his Encounter Report;

'At this distance I could readily see the similarity between the aircraft and the recognition plates of the Me 262. With full power on and the advantage of altitude, I gradually started closing on the enemy aircraft and drew up to within 500 yards astern. I was about to open fire when the enemy pilot cut his throttle and crash-landed in a ploughed field.'

Myers may have scored hits on the engines and cockpit, and the rest of his flight strafed the jet as the pilot ran away. In his Claim Report Myers stated that 2Lt Croy had hit the German pilot, Oberfeldwebel Hieronymous Lauer from 3./KG 51, as he ran away from the burning jet and claimed shared credit with Croy. Lauer escaped the incident uninjured, however, and returned to his unit that night. Myers and Croy were awarded a half credit each in the destruction of the first Me 262 downed by the Allies.

At the end of his Claim Report, Maj Myers described the overall shape and size of the jet, noting what was similar to and different from the published recognition plates that were being used at the time. He stated the chord of the wing, especially at the root, was wider than what was shown on the drawings and the nose was about the same size as that of a P-38, but not as pointed as on the recognition drawings. Where the drawings were correct were the fuselage, engine nacelles and the tail. Finally, he said the overall size of the Me 262 appeared to be the same as a P-38 and looked similar to the B-26 Marauder when viewed from directly above.

Prior to this engagement, Maj Myers had scored three victories flying P-38s with the 55th FG, and he claimed his final success – a Bf 109 – on 7 October 1944, thus falling just a half-kill short of acedom. This Me 262 was Croy's first victory, and he would later claim two Bf 109s on 26 November 1944. On 16 April 1945 Capt Croy was shot down and killed while strafing Straubing airfield.

CHAPTER THREE

BATTLES INTENSIFY

After an eventful four weeks where the USAAF had claimed five victories over the Me 163 and Me 262 in three combats, the next encounter would not take place until 2 October – and this time it would involve pilots from the Ninth Air Force. Although the P-47 groups of the Ninth were tasked primarily with close air support of ground troops, the Thunderbolt pilots still claimed their share of victories.

On the 2nd, 21-year-old Capt Valmore J Beaudrault of Milford, New Hampshire, who had one aerial victory to his name, was leading a flight of 365th FG Thunderbolts on a reconnaissance mission near Münster and Dusseldorf. Flying at 9000 ft, Beaudrault suddenly heard his element leader, 1Lt Robert Teeter, call out over the radio, 'My God. What was that?!' Instinctively checking his tail, Beaudrault spotted something streak past the rear of his fighter and disappear into the clouds. He had never seen anything fly that fast, but his flight gave chase nevertheless. When they popped out on top of the overcast they saw nothing. The P-47 pilots descended through the clouds again to resume their mission, at which point Beaudrault spotted the jet at 'ten o'clock low' and dived in pursuit.

The pilot of Me 262A-1a Wk-Nr 170069 was none other than Oberfeldwebel Hieronymous Lauer, who had been lucky to survive his shoot-down by Lt Col Myers and 2Lt Croy on 28 August. Lauer spotted the three P-47s (one had become separated in the clouds) and accelerated out of range, before turning to engage the fighters head on. The American

Capt 'Chuck' Yeager was at the controls of P-51D-15 44-14888 *GLAMOROUS GLEN III* when he clashed with Me 262s on 6 November 1944. He also used the fighter to down four Fw 190s exactly three weeks later, their destruction taking his final tally to 11.5 victories. Upon his repatriation home in January 1945 the aircraft was passed to fellow ace Capt Don McGee and renamed *Whole Hawg*. On 2 March the fighter was lost to flak along with its pilot, Flt Off Patrick Mallione *(Tony Holmes)*

Capt Valmore J Beaudrault stands with his crew in front of his P-47D-28 44-19713 *Miss Pussy "IV"* at A68 Juvincourt, in France, in the autumn of 1944. These men are, from left to right, Assistant Crew Chief Sgt 'Cactus' Garner, Capt Beaudrault, Crew Chief SSgt Bruno Kupis and Armourer Cpl Mort Sherrod. Ninth Air Force P-47s were primarily tasked with supporting ground troops, but they still scored their share of aerial victories. On 2 October 1944, Beaudrault engaged and shot down a Me 262 near Münster – this was the first jet shot down by a Ninth Air Force fighter, and the first of four Me 262s claimed by the 365th FG. After surviving 73 combat missions and a near fatal crash-landing Capt Beaudrault was assigned to the 87th Infantry Division as an air liaison officer and subsequently fought in the Battle of the Bulge (*Priscilla Beaudrault*)

pilots also turned to fire at the Me 262, at which point Lauer zoomed to altitude to gain separation, before turning to re-engage. Once again the P-47s broke into the attack and the jet overshot. The fight turned into a classic scissors engagement that ended up on the deck with Lauer out of altitude and airspeed. Beaudrault then noticed white puffs coming from the Me 262's engines, and he surmised that the jet had either flamed out or run out of fuel. As Beaudrault closed in on the hapless Me 262, Lauer took evasive action by kicking the rudder, but in doing so his wingtip struck the ground and the aeroplane cartwheeled into a fireball. Incredibly, Lauer survived the crash, albeit with serious injuries that left his hospitalised for four months.

Although Beaudrault never 'made ace', his victory on 2 October was significant because it was the first jet to fall to the guns of a Ninth Air Force fighter, and he was awarded a Distinguished Flying Cross following his success.

Five days later, the first Me 262s being flown exclusively as fighters would fall in combat with the USAAF. Although the Messerschmitt's first flight with all-turbojet power had taken place as long ago as 26 June 1943, the Me 262 had not been tested as a fighter under operational conditions until EKdo 262 was formed in August 1944 under the command of Hauptmann Horst Geyer. This unit consisted of three *Einsatzkommandos* that were located at Lechfeld, Rechlin-Larz, and Erfurt-Bindersleben. In September 1944, General Adolf Galland took the staff section of EKdo 262 and used it as the core of the new III. *Gruppe Erganzungsjagdgeschwader* 2 at Lechfeld. This unit was to oversee all training for the Luftwaffe's jet fighter pilots. The remainder of the unit was transferred to airfields at Hesepe and Achmer, where they would begin intensive operations against Allied heavy bombers.

At that time Galland requested that one of the Luftwaffe's highest-scoring aces of the Eastern Front, Major Walter Nowotny (with 255 victories to his name), command the new unit. Dubbed *Kommando* 'Nowotny', the unit had 30 Me 262A-1s when it formed, but only 15 pilots qualified to fly the jet.

On 7 October 1944, the Eighth Air Force launched more than 1400 heavy bombers, escorted by 900 fighters, against oil industry targets in Politz, Ruhland, Merseburg and Lützkendorf. The day started off well for *Kommando* 'Nowotny' when high-scoring ace Leutnant Franz Schall and future ace Feldwebel Heinz Lennartz scored the unit's first victories with a B-24 apiece. However, the escorts would soon exact a high price for these successes, with three Me 262s falling to American fighters in little more than an hour.

On this mission Maj Richard E Conner was leading 'Black' Section, which consisted of two flights of four P-47Ds from the 82nd FS/78th FG. At 1220 hrs the eight fighters had just rendezvoused with their bombers when Conner led them to an area southwest of Hanover to investigate a report of bandits. Whilst flying at 24,000 ft Conner noticed two unidentified aircraft some 10,000 ft below him, and when he bounced the bandits they both outran his Thunderbolt. It was only then that Conner realised he was chasing a pair of Me 262s. According to his Claim Report, he seemed to think that the jets would accelerate out of range and then turn to re-engage him in an attempt to get a head-on shot, which could be dangerous due to the Me 262's armament of four 30 mm cannon. When the jets did indeed turn back in Conner's direction, he banked tightly inside one of them and opened fire;

'I got several strikes with a 90-degree deflection shot. The enemy aircraft headed for the airdrome and I headed for him at full power. Suddenly he slowed and put down his wheels. I got a dead astern shot, getting strikes, and then overran him. I had to take evasive action from intense, accurate light flak on the drome.'

After Conner overshot the jet, 1Lts Allen A Rosenblum and Robert H Anderson confirmed their section leader's victory when they saw the Me 262 crash and explode on the airfield. Rosenblum and Anderson would later claim their own Me 262 victories in March 1945. This success brought Conner's score to 1.5, and he would survive the war just a half-victory short of being an ace (he was also credited with 3.5 strafing kills). Although it is not definitive, Conner's victim may have been Hauptmann Heinz Arnold, who already had 42 victories to his name when he joined *Kommando* 'Nowotny' from 10./JG 5 on the Eastern Front. Arnold would later become a jet ace, claiming seven victories in the Me 262 with 11./JG 7 in March 1945. He was killed in combat on 17 April.

On 7 October 1944, Maj Richard E Conner from the 82nd FS/78th FG bounced a pair of Me 262s that quickly out-accelerated him. However, one of the German pilots inexplicably turned back into Conner, which allowed him to cut inside the jet's turn and score hits from 90 degrees deflection. When the fighter attempted to land Conner hammered the jet again, sending it down in flames on the edge of an airfield. The pilot is believed to have been 42-victory ace Hauptmann Heinz Arnold, who had claimed seven kills in the Me 262 with 11./JG 7. Conner finished the war with 4.5 aerial victories to his name (© *IWM FRE 3019*)

As of October 1944, USAAF fighters had shot down three Me 163s and three Me 262s, but conspicuously absent from the victor list was the mighty Mustang. This all changed on 7 October when 1Lt Urban 'Ben' Drew of the 375th FS/361st FG shot down two Me 262s that were taking off from Achmer. The gun camera in P-51D-10 44-14164 *DETROIT Miss* failed and his wingman had been shot down and taken prisoner, so confirmation was impossible. However, due to his access to top-secret intelligence reports, Lt Gen 'Jimmy' Doolittle, commander of the Eighth Air Force, personally confirmed Drew's victories (*Boom Powell*)

1Lt Urban 'Ben' Drew of the 375th FS/361st FG had had his first encounter with an Me 262 near Hamm, Germany, in September. Although his Mustang had hit 500 mph when pursuing the jet (almost certainly a bomber from KG 51) in a dive from 20,000 ft, he could not get sufficiently close enough to the aeroplane to open fire. It was a frustrating and sobering experience. On 7 October, Drew was at the controls of P-51D 44-14164 *DETROIT Miss* leading 'Decoy Squadron' on a mission escorting 3rd Air Division B-17s attacking oil industry targets in the Böhlen/Lützkendorf area. He had taken his flight beneath the bombers to engage enemy fighters that had been intercepted by other escorts, but by the time they arrived on the scene all the aircraft had disappeared. Unable to locate his original B-17s, Drew joined a box of homebound red-tailed Flying Fortresses that were short on escorts. However, he was still on the hunt for that all-important fifth victory – his tally then stood at four aerial kills (and one strafing victory). Drew knew that this mission would take him to the same area where he had encountered the Me 262s a few weeks prior. His eagerness paid off.

Approximately 75 minutes after Conner's victory near Hanover, Drew neared Achmer airfield just as ace Oberleutnant Paul Bley took off in Me 262A-1a Wk-Nr 110405, with fellow ace Leutnant Gerhard Kobert on his wing in Me 262A-1a Wk-Nr 170307 and future ace Oberfähnrich Heinz Russel about to commence his takeoff run. Drew had been watching Bley and Kobert from 15,000 ft, and when they took off he rolled in on them, with 2Lts Bob McCandliss and Bill McCoppin on his wing. When Drew levelled off at tree-top height, his closure speed was so great that he was suddenly concerned about overshooting. Flak from the airfield was also heavy and accurate. Drew later noted in his Encounter Report;

'I caught up with the second ME-262 when he was about 1000 ft off the ground. I was indicating 450 mph and the jet aircraft could not have been going over 200 mph. I started firing from about 400 yards, with 30 degrees of deflection, and as I closed on him I observed hits all over the fuselage and wings.'

Suddenly, Leutnant Kobert's jet exploded, forcing Drew to fly right through the fireball and debris. Once clear of the conflagration, he briefly glanced back over his shoulder to watch his first victim go in, before focusing his attention on Oberleutnant Bley. The latter had already made a fatal mistake, as Drew related to 'Boom' Powell, author of his biography, *Ben Drew – The Katzenjammer Ace*, in 1986;

'He turned. To this day I don't know why. The best I can figure is he reverted to old habits and turned into his attacker – me. When an enemy's nose was pointed at you, you turned. If he had kept accelerating he would have outrun me.'

The jet was already 60 degrees angle off and Drew was still doing more than 400 mph when he rolled into a 90-degree left bank and put 6Gs on *DETROIT Miss*. Drew grunted as sweat poured into his eyes, his mask began to droop around his chin and his vision went grey. The Gs were painful, but he kept pulling as the pipper of his K-14 gunsight began gaining on the German fighter. Drew's vision was now beginning to narrow, and he knew that if he kept the Gs on he would black out in just a few seconds. At that moment he managed to place the pipper over the tail of the jet. He immediately opened fire, 'walking' the tracer rounds up the fuselage and into the cockpit, shattering the canopy. The jet went into an inverted spin and struck the ground at a 60-degree angle. Amazingly, Oberleutnant Bley, a Bf 110 ace with eight victories to his name, successfully bailed out of the stricken jet, only to die a few weeks later in a takeoff accident.

In less than 60 seconds 'Ben' Drew had shot down two of Hitler's elite jet fighters. However, his euphoria was short-lived, for the P-51 of his wingman, Bob McCandliss, had been struck by flak, forcing him to bail out of his burning Mustang just seconds before it hit the ground. There was handshaking and backslapping all around when Drew landed back at the 361st FG's Bottisham, Cambridgeshire, home, but before he could celebrate he needed confirmation of his kills. This initially proved difficult to achieve for the new colour gun camera film loaded in *DETROIT Miss* had failed, McCandliss was a PoW and McCoppin had been too busy strafing flak batteries to notice either jet go in. However, confirmation eventually came from Lt Gen 'Jimmy' Doolittle, commander of the Eighth Air Force, who had access to top-secret intelligence reports noting the demise of two Me 262s on this date.

Exactly a week after Maj Conner scored the 78th FG's second Me 262 victory, 2Lt Huie H Lamb was flying as wingman for Capt John I Brown when he downed the I./KG 51 Me 262A-1a flown by Fahnenjunker-Feldwebel Edgar Junghans near Bohmte. This victory marked the last jet kill scored by the 78th FG whilst flying the P-47. Although Lamb fell 2.5 victories short of 'making ace', he claimed a share in the destruction of an Ar 234 with 1Lt Allen A Rosenblum on 19 March 1945, which placed him in the fairly exclusive club of 13 USAAF pilots that scored multiple jet victories. Rosenblum joined the same club three days later when he shared

In this publicity shot of 1Lt Drew and his Crew Chief, SSgt Vernon Davis, the canopy rail on *DETROIT Miss* displays 'Ben's' final tally of seven victories – six aerial and one strafing. Drew was the first of only two USAAF pilots to shoot down a pair of jets in a single engagement (*Boom Powell*)

On 2 November 1944 Capt Freddie Glover was leading the 4th FG's 336th FS on an escort mission when the bombers were attacked by Me 163s. One of the rocket fighters literally flew right in front of Glover, who, after a quick turn, fired a burst that set the Komet on fire. The pilot, Leutnant Günter Andreas of 2./JG 400, duly bailed out. Glover was at the controls of this P-51D-5 (44-13317) when he downed the Komet, the fighter being assigned to Capt Donald Emerson when photographed here at Debden in August 1944 (*Courtesy of Donald Pierini, Sr*)

On the same mission during which Glover scored his victory, Capt Louis 'Red Dog' Norley, Operations Officer for the 335th FS/4th FG, engaged a Komet from a distance of just 50 yards. Scoring many hits before overshooting, Norley repositioned himself for another attacking pass. He achieved more good strikes from 400 yards that caused the Komet to roll over and go straight in from 8000 ft. Unlike Glover's victim, the pilot of the Me 163, Oberfeldwebel Jakob Bollenrath from 1./JG 400, was killed

an Me 262 with Capt Winfield Brown. Lamb and Rosenblum both finished the war with 2.5 aerial victories, with the former also destroying three aircraft on the ground and the latter, one.

On 1 November two flights of P-51s from the 335th FS/4th FG, led by Capt Louis 'Red Dog' Norley, were escorting two B-24 combat wings to Gelsenkirchen when they had a brief encounter with a trio of Me 262s as the Liberators dropped their bombs at 1420 hrs. The group's Intelligence Report stated, 'A little later some encounter was experienced with a jet Me-262. As this first jet made its attack, two more 262s appeared on the scene but they turned away and ran as our fighters turned into them. The jets could not be overtaken'.

The next day, nearly the entire 4th FG was airborne escorting Eighth Air Force bombers to Merseburg. Again, Capt Norley, flying P-51D 44-15028 was leading 22 P-51s of the 335th FS, while Capt Freddie Glover led a similar number of Mustangs from the 336th. JG 400 attempted to intercept the Merseburg-bound bombers, launching more than 15 Komets in what would be the unit's largest mission of the war.

At 1410 hrs Capt Glover was leading the group south of Leipzig just under a ten-tenths overcast at 25,000 ft when he noticed a contrail climbing up from east to west just as the first box of bombers were dropping their ordnance;

'The contrail cut off at bomber level, which was about 25,000 ft. As it cut off I could distinguish an aircraft. The aircraft made a 180-degree starboard turn and headed back east in a slight dive. I dropped my tanks and headed for it on a converging course. The aircraft headed east, and myself north. As the aircraft crossed in front of me I recognised it to be a Me 163 Rocket Ship. I made a quick 90-degree turn to the east and dropped in line astern. I opened fire immediately from a range of about 400 yards. I got immediate strikes on the tail, wings and cockpit. The belly of the Me 163 caught first and exploded.'

When the Komet exploded, Glover overshot and came back around to observe the rocket fighter wallowing, burning and shedding pieces. He broke left as more Me 163s were coming up, so he did not see Leutnant Günter Andreas of 2./JG 400 bail out of the stricken Komet.

Just after Glover sent Andreas' Komet down in flames, Capt Norley latched onto the tail of the Me 163 flown by Oberfeldwebel Jakob Bollenrath of 1./JG 400;

'I was leading "Caboose Squadron" at 25,000 ft under the layer [of cloud] southeast of the target. We were just completing a port orbit, waiting for the jets to come down, when one did pop out at "six o'clock" to me. I immediately dropped my tanks, advancing full boost and revs. I set my gyro sight for 30 ft and closed the graticule [sic] to maximum range. I encountered no difficulty in putting the dot on the jet. However, I was quite a little out of range – about 1000 yards. I got on the jet's tail and followed him down.

'The jet started pulling away from me, so I fired a few short bursts hoping to make him turn, whereby I could possibly cut him off and get in range. The jet did start to level out and make a port turn – his speed dropped off considerably and his turn increased. I closed on him very rapidly. I was using a K-14 gunsight for the first time and do not remember opening the graticule as I closed in. However, I did get a couple of strikes on his tail, ranging from 280 yards down to 50 yards, ten degrees off. My speed was approximately 450 mph when I got into range. I throttled back but was too fast to stay in the turn with him due to my excessive speed. I overshot him, pulled up and got on his tail again.

'Up to this time the jet had not been using his blower – at least he was not emitting any black smoke. As I closed on him the second time he used his blower for a couple of seconds and then cut it off again. I closed to 400 yards from 20 degrees off, fired again and saw strikes on the tail. The jet rolled over and started straight down from 8000 ft, with fire coming intermittently from his port side and exhaust. He crashed in a small village and exploded.'

This was the last large-scale mission undertaken by JG 400, which from this point on was not an effective fighting force. Aside from the aeroplanes claimed by the 4th FG, Oberfeldwebel Herbert Straznicky was lost when his Komet crashed during the mission (he too was probably shot down, although there were no claims made by USAAF fighters for a third Me 163 kill) and 36-victory ace Oberfeldwebel Horst Rolly died when his parachute failed after he bailed out of his Komet when it burst into flames shortly after takeoff. Bollenrath's Me 163, therefore, was the last one to be shot down by the USAAF.

Although the two Komets claimed on 2 November were the first of 11 jet victories that would be scored by the 4th FG, they were the only such kills that either Glover or Norley would make. The Me 163 raised Capt Glover's score to 6.333, and he would finish the war a double ace with 10.333 aerial and 14.5 strafing victories to his name. The Komet credited to Capt Norley brought his score to 8.333 aerial victories, and he too would end his tour in the ETO with 10.333 aerial (and five strafing) victories.

The area around Osnabrück was fast becoming a hotbed of jet activity, and that is precisely where 357th FG pilots Capt Charles 'Chuck' Yeager and 1Lts William Quinn and James Kenney each downed an Me 262 on 6 November. Leading 'White' Flight at 8000 ft just north of Osnabrück, Yeager spotted three Me 262s in a 'V' formation on a reciprocal course to the Mustangs just above a broken layer of cloud at 5000 ft. As Yeager took his flight down the jets took no evasive action, even after he had achieved one or two hits with a 90-degree deflection shot from 400 yards. Yeager felt that the German pilots were relying on their superior speed to outrun the Mustangs. It worked, as the jets disappeared into a haze layer.

Undeterred, Yeager dropped down through the haze, and after about a minute he met the jets again head-on, with the Me 262s slightly below him at 2000 ft. He split-essed down and got the flight leader in his sights, scoring several hits on the wings and fuselage, but the jet still managed to pull away and disappear into the haze again.

By now Yeager had become separated from his flight, and as he climbed back up to 8000 ft he spotted a large airfield, which he began to circle. His persistent hunting instincts paid off;

'I spotted a lone 262 approaching the field from the south at 500 ft. It was going very slow – around 200 mph. I split-essed on it and was

Some Me 163s had a narrow escape. This photograph was taken with the gun camera fitted to Capt W H Anderson's P-51D of the 335th FS during the mission led by Capt Norley on 2 November 1944. Although damaged, the Me 163 was not shot down (*JG 400 Archive*)

Capt (seen here as a 1Lt) 'Chuck' Yeager of the 363rd FS/357th FG claimed one Me 262 destroyed and two damaged near Osnabrück on 6 November 1944 (© *IWM FRE 3128*)

going around 500 mph at 500 ft. Flak started coming up very thick and accurate. I fired a short burst from around 400 yards and got hits on the wings. I had to break off at 300 yards because the flak was getting too close. Looking back, I saw the jet enemy aircraft crash-land about 400 yards short of the airfield in a wooded field.'

The Me 262 was Yeager's seventh victory, and he would finish his tour with 11.5 aerial kills. He was also credited with damaging two more Messerschmitt jets during this clash.

On the afternoon of 8 November, pilots from the 364th FG were escorting B-17s that were returning from Merseburg when they heard a call that bombers were under attack in the vicinity of Dummer Lake, ten miles north of Osnabrück. In the ensuing dogfight, 2Lt Richard W Stevens of the 384th FS, flying P-51D 44-14093, shot down an Me 262 from *Kommando* 'Nowotny'. In the next ten minutes two more jets from the unit would fall to Eighth Air Force Mustangs, but the final loss of the day was one from which the unit would not recover.

The 364th FS/357th FG had been strafing targets west of Hanover, and during these attacks Capt Merle Allen and his wingman, 1Lt Edward Haydon, became separated from the rest of the squadron. The pair were heading west towards England when they spotted a single Me 262 and gave chase. Although they could not have known it at the time, this jet was being flown by none other than Major Walter Nowotny, who had just scored his 257th (B-17) and

1Lt Ernest C 'Feeb' Fiebelkorn of the 77th FS/20th FG scored his nine aerial victories in five engagements between 14 July and 8 November 1944. This photograph was taken at Kings Cliffe just after Fiebelkorn had almost become an 'Ace in a Day' on 28 September when he shot down three Bf 109s and an Fw 190 and damaged another Bf 109 over Magdeburg. Although he returned home in December 1944, Fiebelkorn ended the war as the highest-scoring ace of the 20th FG (*20th FW Association*)

'Feeb' Fiebelkorn's final victory of the war, claimed in his assigned P-51D-5 44-11161 *June Nite,* was a shared victory with 1Lt Edward Haydon of the 364th FS/357th FG on 8 November 1944. Their victim was none other than Major Walter Nowotny, who, just moments before, had scored his 257th (B-17) and 258th (P-51) aerial victories. Fiebelkorn went on to fly F-82 Twin Mustangs in Korea with the 4th FS/51st FG, where he and his Radar Observer, Capt John J Higgins, were killed whilst undertaking a close air support mission on 6 July 1950. After his remains were located in 1953, Capt Ernest Fiebelkorn was buried in the Arlington National Cemetery in Virginia (*Peter Randall collection*)

258th (P-51) aerial victories. There were several other Mustangs chasing Nowotny, including Capt Ernest C Fiebelkorn of the 77th FS/20th FG, who was flying his assigned P-51D 44-11161 *June Nite*. He filed the following report;

'I was leading "Yellow" Flight in the vicinity of Dummer Lake when an Me 262 came down by my flight. I immediately started after the jet and followed it in a dive to near the deck, where the jet levelled out. At this time there were quite a few other P-51s starting after the 262. The jet led us across an airdrome in a gradual turn and I was cutting inside just within range when two P-51s from a group believed to be the 357th cut me out before I could fire. The jet pulled up into overcast, but immediately came down again on its back and crashed into the ground about four-five miles from the airdrome.'

In this engagement only 1Lt Haydon actually fired on Nowotny's Me 262. Capt Allen did not file a claim because he never opened fire, but as it can be seen in his Encounter Report, Fiebelkorn did not fire either, but he ended up sharing credit with Haydon for downing one of the Luftwaffe's top aces. This was Haydon's only victory of the war and the ninth, and last, aerial success for Capt Fiebelkorn, who also had two strafing kills.

Walter Nowotny's demise sounded the death knell for the unit that bore his name. After Hitler finally gave permission for the Me 262 to be built as a fighter instead of a bomber, General Galland moved forward with the organisation of JG 7 'Nowotny'. The world's first jet fighter unit of any size and significance, JG 7 would be credited with almost 300 aerial victories during its seven-month defence of the Reich.

For the rest of November and during December four Me 262s fell to non-aces. On 9 December Stabsfeldwebel Hans Zander of 4./KG 51 was shot down and killed by 2Lt Harry L Edwards of the 486th FS/352nd FG – this aeroplane was Edwards' first of two victories. Then on 22 December 1Lt Eugene P McGlauflin and 2Lt Roy L Scales, both from the Italy-based 308th FS/31st FG, shared in the destruction of the first Me 262 to fall to the guns of the Fifteenth Air Force.

In an effort to build up the tactical air forces covering the frontlines, the 352nd FG forward deployed to Y29 Asch, in Belgium, on 23 December

1Lt John C Meyer was 24 years old when he was given command of the 34th (later redesignated the 487th) FS in December 1942. He scored his, and the 352nd FG's, first aerial victory during the group's combat debut on 26 November 1943. Meyer's final victories were claimed on New Year's Day 1945 during the famous dogfight known as the 'Legend of Y29', bringing his overall tally to 24 aerial and 13 strafing victories. Meyer remained in the service and saw more combat in the Korean War, where he flew 31 missions in F-86 Sabres whilst leading the 4th FIG. During his tour he shot down two MiG-15s and damaged a third. Meyer rose through the general ranks while serving in such posts as Vice-Chief of Staff of the USAF and commanding general of Strategic Air Command, eventually attaining the rank of general prior to his retirement in July 1974 (*352nd FG Association*)

1944 due to its close proximity to the frontlines – then, just 15 miles away. While here, the group would operate under the command of the Ninth Air Force. On 31 December, Lt Col John C Meyer, deputy CO of the 352nd, was leading the 328th FS on a patrol when fighter controllers vectored them towards a group of bogies near Viviers. When the Mustang pilots dropped below the clouds they spotted an Ar 234 bomber, which was quickly attacked by ace Capt Donald S Bryan, who stated that he got good hits on the starboard engine prior to breaking off his pursuit when Lt Col Meyer saw a second Arado closing in on Bryan's tail.

Meyer duly chased the second bomber in and out of the clouds until he lost sight of it near Bonn. Just as he spotted it again, he noticed another Ar 234 heading towards Cologne, and gave chase. Meyer fired several bursts from long range, and even though he observed no hits, he claimed, and was awarded, credit for downing the first Ar 234 to fall to the USAAF. The Arado was the 22nd of 24 aerial victories scored by Meyer in World War 2 – he also claimed 13 strafing kills.

On 31 December 1944, Lt Col Meyer led the 328th FS on a patrol in P-51D-15 44-15041 *PETIE 3rd*, his final Mustang. During the mission Meyer chased an Ar 234 that ultimately escaped. He subsequently spotted a second Arado bomber near Cologne and fired several long-range bursts during an extended chase, being duly credited with the USAAF's first Ar 234 victory (*352nd FG Association*)

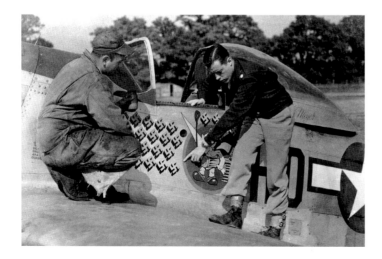

Although not as photographed as the more famous P-51D-10 44-14151 *PETIE 2nd*, Lt Col Meyer scored more victories in *PETIE 3rd* than any of his previous Mustangs (or his solitary Thunderbolt). In this publicity photograph Meyer inspects the latest kill markings applied to *PETIE 3rd* by his crew chief, SSgt W N Conkey (*352nd FG Association*

COLOUR PLATES

1
P-38L-15 42-104425 *BOOMERANG* of Capt Arthur Jeffrey,
434th FS/479th FG, Wattisham, July 1944

2
P-47D-28 44-19713 *Miss Pussy "IV"* of Capt Valmore Beaudrault, 386th FS/365th FG,
A68 Juvincourt, Belgium, October 1944

3
P-51D-10 44-14164 *DETROIT Miss* of 1Lt Urban 'Ben' Drew,
375th FS/361st FG, Little Walden, October 1944

4
P-47D-28 42-28442 of 2Lt Huie Lamb, 82nd FS/78th FG,
Duxford, October 1944

5
P-51D-5 44-13317 of Capt Freddie Glover, 336th FS/4th FG,
Debden, November 1944

6
P-51D-15 44-15028 *Red Dog* of Capt Louis Norley, 335th FS/4th FG,
Debden, November 1944

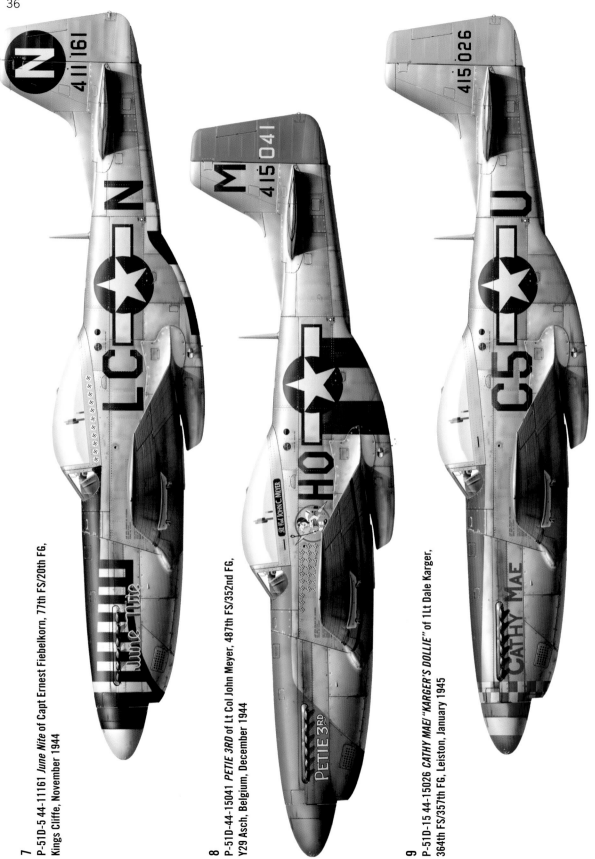

7
P-51D-5 44-11161 *June Nite* of Capt Ernest Fiebelkorn, 77th FS/20th FG,
Kings Cliffe, November 1944

8
P-51D-44-15041 *PETIE 3RD* of Lt Col John Meyer, 487th FS/352nd FG,
Y29 Asch, Belgium, December 1944

9
P-51D-15 44-15026 *CATHY MAE! "KARGER'S DOLLIE"* of 1Lt Dale Karger,
364th FS/357th FG, Leiston, January 1945

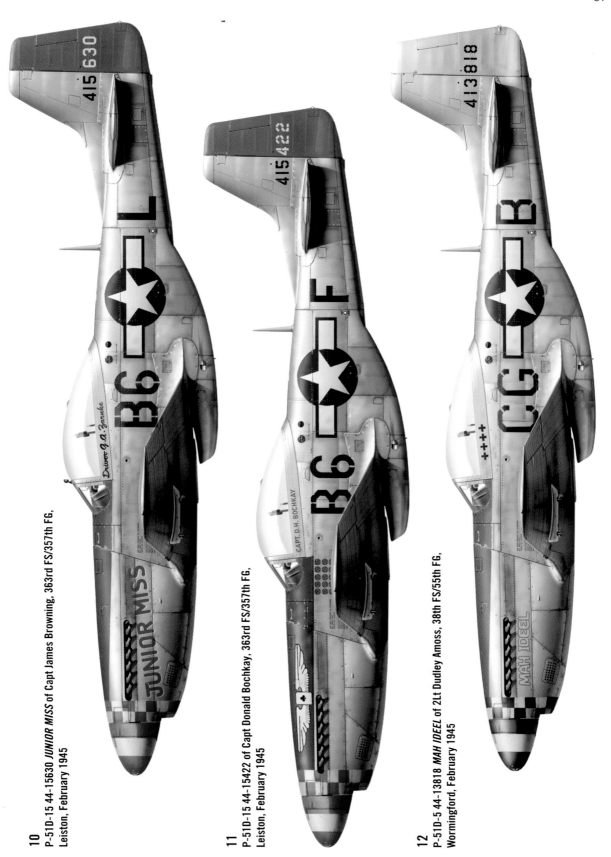

10
P-51D-15 44-15630 *JUNIOR MISS* of Capt James Browning, 363rd FS/357th FG,
Leiston, February 1945

11
P-51D-15 44-15422 of Capt Donald Bochkay, 363rd FS/357th FG,
Leiston, February 1945

12
P-51D-5 44-13818 *MAH IDEEL* of 2Lt Dudley Amoss, 38th FS/55th FG,
Wormingford, February 1945

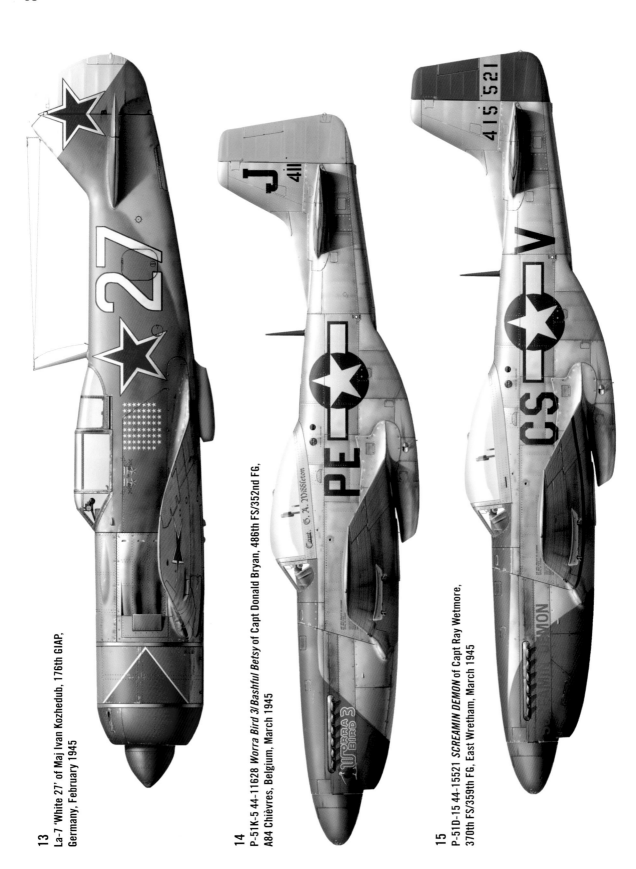

13
La-7 'White 27' of Maj Ivan Kozhedub, 176th GIAP,
Germany, February 1945

14
P-51K-5 44-11628 *Worra Bird 3*/*Bashful Betsy* of Capt Donald Bryan, 486th FS/352nd FG,
A84 Chièvres, Belgium, March 1945

15
P-51D-15 44-15521 *SCREAMIN DEMON* of Capt Ray Wetmore,
370th FS/359th FG, East Wretham, March 1945

16
P-51D-15 44-15717 *WILD WILL* of Maj Niven Cranfill, 368th FS/359th FG,
East Wretham, March 1945

17
P-51D 44-63621 *LITTLE SHRIMP* of Maj Robert Foy,
363rd FS/357th FG, Leiston, March 1945

18
P-51D (sub-type and serial number unknown) *BUNNIE* of 1Lt Roscoe Brown,
100th FS/332nd FG, Ramitelli, Italy, March 1945

19
P-47M-1 44-21160 "*Devastatin Deb*" of Maj George Bostwick and
Capt John Fahringer, 63rd FS/56th FG, Boxted, March/April 1945

20
P-51D-20 44-63668 *LIVE BAIT* of Capt Clayton Gross, 355th FS/354th FG,
Y64 Ober Olm, Germany, April 1945

21
P-51D-20 44-64147 *BIG DICK* of Capt Richard Hewitt,
82nd FS/78th FG, Duxford, April 1945

22
P-47D-28 42-28453 *The Irish Shillalah* of 1Lt James Finnegan, 10th FS/50th FG,
Y90 Giebelstadt, Germany, April 1945

23
Tempest V JN817/JF-H of Flt Lt A E Umbers, No 3 Sqn, B80 Volkel, Holland, 21 October 1944

24
Tempest V EJ750/JBW of Wg Cdr J B Wray, No 122 Wing,
B80 Volkel, Holland, November–December 1944

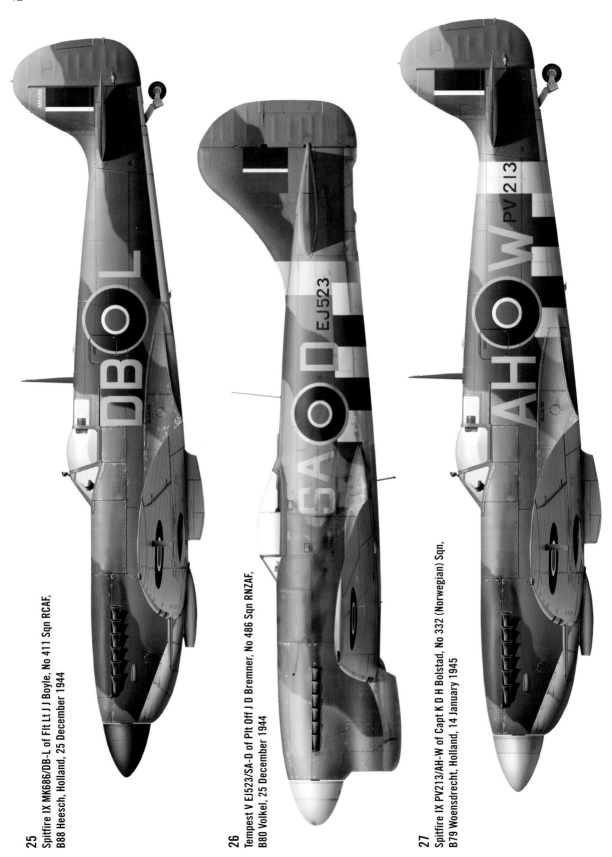

25
Spitfire IX MK686/DB-L of Flt Lt I J Boyle, No 411 Sqn RCAF,
B88 Heesch, Holland, 25 December 1944

26
Tempest V EJ523/SA-D of Plt Off J D Bremner, No 486 Sqn RNZAF,
B80 Volkel, 25 December 1944

27
Spitfire IX PV213/AH-W of Capt K D H Bolstad, No 332 (Norwegian) Sqn,
B79 Woensdrecht, Holland, 14 January 1945

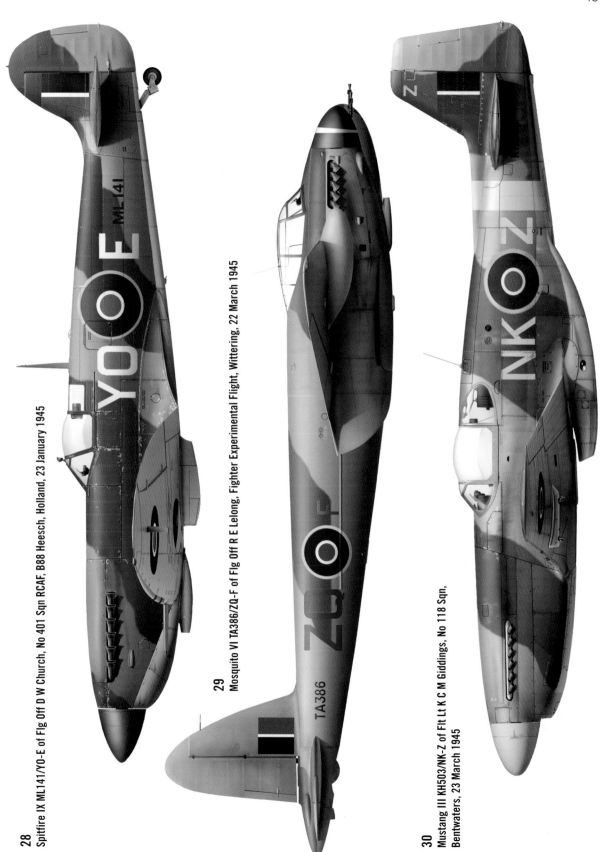

28
Spitfire IX ML141/YO-E of Flg Off D W Church, No 401 Sqn RCAF, B88 Heesch, Holland, 23 January 1945

29
Mosquito VI TA386/ZQ-F of Flg Off R E Lelong, Fighter Experimental Flight, Wittering, 22 March 1945

30
Mustang III KH503/NK-Z of Flt Lt K C M Giddings, No 118 Sqn, Bentwaters, 23 March 1945

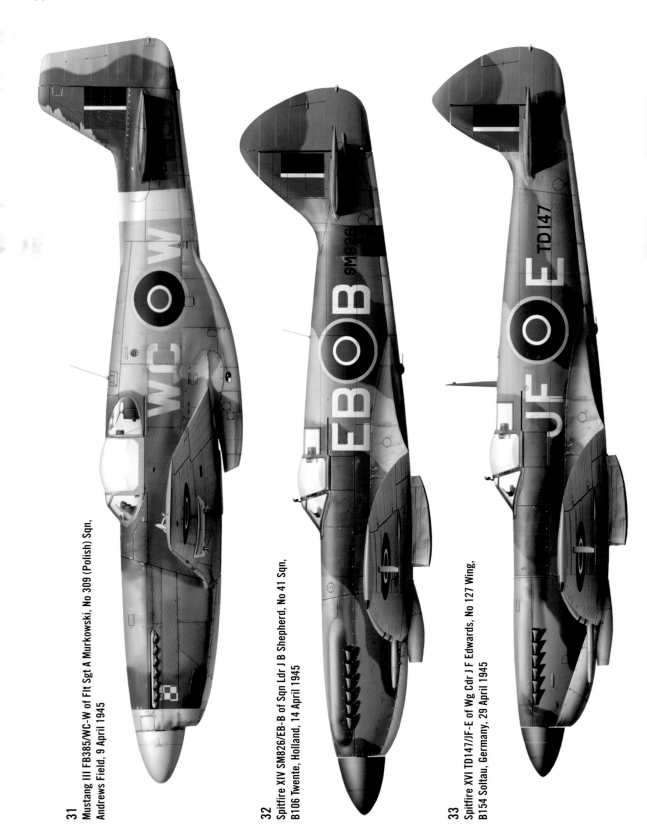

31
Mustang III FB385/WC-W of Flt Sgt A Murkowski, No 309 (Polish) Sqn,
Andrews Field, 9 April 1945

32
Spitfire XIV SM826/EB-B of Sqn Ldr J B Shepherd, No 41 Sqn,
B106 Twente, Holland, 14 April 1945

33
Spitfire XVI TD147/JF-E of Wg Cdr J F Edwards, No 127 Wing,
B154 Soltau, Germany, 29 April 1945

CHAPTER FOUR

BODENPLATTE TO VARSITY

On 9 February 1945, the 363rd FS/ 357th FG had escorted 3rd Air Division B-17s to Fulda. Seven-victory ace Capt James W Browning was leading a flight of Mustangs in P-51D-15 44-15630 *JUNIOR MISS*, which was usually flown by 1Lt Glenwood A Zarnke. Browning's wingman was fellow ace Capt Donald H Bochkay in his P-51D-15 44-15422. When four Me 262s were spotted 4000 ft below their flight, Browning and Bochkay bounced them, with each pilot going after two jets. The outcome of the ensuing engagement would be vastly different for each pilot (*Lt Col Clarence 'Bud' Anderson*)

New Year's Day 1945 is best known as the date the Luftwaffe launched low-level attacks on 21 Allied airfields in northwest Europe. Codenamed Operation *Bodenplatte*, the Germans sent aloft more than 900 aircraft, including Me 262s and Ar 234s from KG 51 and KG 76, respectively. The pilots of JG 7 were not involved, however, as they were held back to defend the Reich from the inevitable retaliatory heavy bomber raids mounted by the Eighth Air Force.

In January 1945 six jets, all Me 262s, were shot down by eight pilots from the 55th, 353rd and 357th FGs, but only two of them were aces – and both were from the 357th FG. During a mission escorting 2nd Air Division Liberators to Leipheim on 15 January 1945, 1Lt Robert P Winks of the 364th FS/357th FG was orbiting over Schongau aerodrome when he spotted an enemy aircraft performing aerobatics directly overhead! In his Encounter Report Winks wrote;

'I sighted an enemy aircraft doing a series of slow rolls on the deck and immediately called it in. No one could locate it, so I went down from 15,000 ft, got on his tail and fired a good burst just as the enemy aircraft was again approaching the airdrome. I observed many strikes and the fuselage burst into flames. The enemy aircraft crashed on the edge of the field and blew up. The pilot was not seen to get out.'

After downing the Me 262, Winks started to climb back up to altitude, but noticed his engine was strangely quiet and the propeller was wind-milling. It was then that he realised he had failed to switch to his internal fuel tanks when he dropped his external tanks as he dived after the jet. Winks was so focused on claiming his ace-making fifth victory that he had failed to notice his Mustang's engine had stopped running! The 357th's newest ace could not identify the aircraft he had shot down when he returned to Leiston, although he was quickly informed that it had in fact been an Me 262.

Five days after 1Lt Winks' victory, the 357th FG was escorting B-17s from the 3rd Air Division deep into southern Germany when again it encountered Me 262s. While the Flying Fortresses attacked the marshalling yards at Heilbronn, 15 miles north of Stuttgart, Mustangs from the 364th FS performed a sweep of the Ulm-Augsburg-Munich area some 50-60 miles southeast of the target area. By this late stage of the war in the ETO, USAAF fighter pilots had been given permission to strafe targets of opportunity. In an area between Ulm and Munich, 19-year-old 1Lt Dale E Karger and his wingman 2Lt Lloyd Zacharie were attacking a train when another pilot from the 364th spotted a pair of contrails in a slow, spiralling, descent from 32,000 ft. Despite still being a teenager, Karger already had four victories to his credit, and recounted the ensuing engagement with the jet;

'I still had my wingman with me, and said over the radio that we would climb up and intercept. As we neared their altitude the two Me 262s headed east, towards the city of Munich, and descended slightly. By this time we were at full throttle, and they were pulling away rapidly.

'As they approached the city, I could see one Me 262 – a mere speck by this time – making a left turn. I immediately turned north in order to cut him off and intercept. Apparently he underestimated me and kept on coming around at a rapid rate. He was now heading west, with me still heading north. As he closed, I started a left turn to line up for a shot. When I got him up in the computing gunsight I could see he was still slightly out of range and moving very fast at my altitude – about 3000 ft. I led him about one-eighth of an inch with the computing gunsight and opened fire. Pieces of his canopy started blowing off, so I must have hit him close to the cockpit.'

A few seconds later Karger watched the pilot bail out of the badly damaged Me 262, which split-essed and crashed in a wooded area. After Karger's engagement the 364th headed back in the direction of the target area, where 1Lt Edward Haydon, who had shot down Maj Nowotny on 8 November 1944, spotted another Me 262 and dived in pursuit of it along with his wingman, 2Lt Roland R Wright. In a brief low-altitude engagement, the latter destroyed the jet (for his first of two aerial victories), but Haydon's Mustang was hit by flak and he barely survived a low-altitude bail out. The Mustang pilot spent the rest of the war as a PoW.

On 9 February, the Eighth Air Force sent 1300 B-17s and B-24s, escorted by more than 850 P-47s and P-51s, to attack synthetic oil plants at Fulda and Lützkendorf, an armament plant in Weimar and railway marshalling yards in Magdeburg. Amongst the fighters scrambled to intercept the bombers were 15 Me 262s from 1./KG(J) 54 – an all-weather unit manned by pilots pulled from Ju 88 and He 111 bomber units. This was to be its combat debut, and for several of the pilots this would be their first, and last, combat sortie in the Me 262.

While on an escort mission to Leipheim on 15 January 1945, 1Lt Robert P Winks of the 364th FS/357th FG was orbiting over Schongau aerodrome when he noticed a jet over the field performing aerobatics. He dropped his external tanks and dived on the Me 262 from an altitude of 15,000 ft, sending it crashing in flames with a well-aimed burst. As Winks climbed back to altitude, he noticed that his engine was silent and his propeller was wind-milling. It was then that he realised he had failed to switch to his internal fuel tanks when he dropped his external tanks as he dived after the jet. Winks had scored his ace-making fifth victory in an unpowered P-51!
(*Lt Col Clarence 'Bud' Anderson*)

One of the escorting pilots was 363rd FS/357th FG ace Capt Donald H Bochkay, flying his assigned P-51D 44-15422 as wingman for fellow ace Capt James W Browning, who was at the controls of 1Lt Glenwood A Zarnke's P-51D 44-15630 *JUNIOR MISS*. The 363rd was escorting a number of 3rd Air Division B-17s to Fulda. At 1145 hrs, a flight of four Me 262s was spotted 4000 ft below the squadron, and Browning and Bochkay dropped their external tanks and went after the jets. The German pilots saw the Mustangs coming down and broke into two pairs, with Browning going after the pair on the left, but they eventually sped out of range.

Bochkay, meanwhile, chased the second pair up to 28,000 ft, and just as they levelled off the German fighters made a steep climbing turn to the right. Their pursuer dived from 'up sun' to cut them off, the Me 262 pilots failing to see Bochkay closing on the lead jet. He duly overshot this aircraft and broke right, coming out on the tail of the wingman. At a range of just 300 yards Bochkay fired a long burst as the Me 262 began to accelerate out of range, but inexplicably the jet then broke left, which allowed him to close in and fire another long burst that shattered the canopy. Suddenly, Bochkay had to break right again to avoid colliding with the now rapidly decelerating jet. The second burst must have killed the pilot because Bochkay spotted him hanging half out of the cockpit, and when the jet rolled onto its back he fell out without opening his parachute. The Me 262 then went into a vertical dive at high speed and crashed.

Bochkay briefly went after another jet that bounced seven Mustangs, but two of his guns then fell silent after firing less than 12 rounds, their ammunition having been exhausted. He then attempted to rejoin Browning but could not locate him, so he joined up with another Mustang from his squadron.

Elsewhere in the skies near Fulda, ace Maj Robert W Foy and his wingman 1Lt Johnnie L Carter bounced two Me 262s from 22,000 ft. While still diving on the jets, which were at 15,000 ft, Foy fired from extreme range and hit the right engine of one of them. Trailing smoke, the jet rolled over into a cloud bank below and Foy was unable to follow it – he was credited with a probable. Carter had better luck because after firing a brief burst and seeing strikes, the pilot (possibly Major Ottfried Sehrt, flying Me 262A-2a Wk-Nr 110799) bailed out and ended up as the only survivor of the four Me 262s that were lost that day. The third jet destroyed fell to 1Lt Stephen C Ananian of the 505th FS/339th FG, this being his only aerial success (he also claimed a strafing victory).

When the pilots of the 363rd FS landed back at Leiston, Browning was not among them. The report for the mission stated, 'One NYR

Capt Donald Bochkay, flying his P-51D-15 44-15422 on 9 February 1945, chased two Me 262s up to 28,000 ft, where he had to break hard to the right to avoid a collision when one of the jets turned suddenly. This manoeuvre put him just 300 yards behind the second jet, which was quickly accelerating. When the Me 262 turned again, Bochkay closed in and fired a burst that shattered the canopy and killed the pilot (*Lt Col Clarence 'Bud' Anderson*)

On 9 February 1945, Maj Robert W Foy (flying this aircraft, P-51D-20 44-63621) and his wingman, 1Lt Johnnie L Carter, attacked a pair of jets at 15,000 ft. Foy scored hits on the right engine of an Me 262, which slowly rolled over into the clouds, where Foy lost sight of it. He claimed a probable. Carter fired several effective bursts at the other Me 262, forcing the pilot to bail out. This was Carter's fourth, and final, victory of the war (*Lt Col Clarence 'Bud' Anderson*)

[Not Yet Returned], Capt Browning, last seen vicinity of Fulda'. His fate remained a mystery for 50 years, some sources alleging he may have been shot down by 45-victory ace Leutnant Karl Schnörrer of 9./JG 7, who claimed 11 kills with the Me 262, but there was no real evidence to support that theory. The truth of Browning's fate was finally uncovered in the early 1990s when Merle Olmsted, a former groundcrewman with the 357th and its official historian, located Browning's Missing Aircrew Report (MACR) in the National Archives. Attached to the MACR were Army transcripts from August 1947 interviews with Adolf Keller, Burgermeister of Wörsdorf, and Wilhelm Manrer, a railway employee, both of whom witnessed a dogfight that day.

Keller told Army investigators, 'I saw a dogfight in the vicinity of Würges [60 miles west of Fulda]. Besides a German fighter that was engaged in the fight, there were several other aeroplanes in the air. The German fighter rammed an aeroplane and both of them caught fire and crashed'. Manrer said he heard the sound of machine guns, followed by an explosion. He went outside and saw a column of smoke about 600 yards from his railway station. Later that afternoon both Keller and Manrer went to the crash site. A feldwebel in the Wehrmacht gave Keller several items from the wreckage of the Mustang, including a gold ring, a dog tag with Browning's name on it, currency and a photograph, also marked with Browning's name. Manrer said the wreckage of the P-51 was spread over an area of about 400 yards, and he found a section of the canopy rail with Zarnke's name on it.

Browning had hit Me 262 Wk-Nr 500042, flown by Oberstleutnant Volprecht Freiherr von Riedesel, commander of KG(J) 54. After they had collided, both aircraft caught fire and spun in, coming down within 600 yards of each other. Riedesel is reported to have survived the crash, but he died in hospital the next day. Unfortunately, there were no recoverable remains of Capt James W Browning, so the 28-year-old seven-victory ace (who also had two strafing kills) is listed on 'The Wall of the Missing' at the American Military Cemetery in Luxembourg.

Six days later, 2Lt Dudley 'Dixie' Amoss of the 38th FS/55th FG was flying one of 500+ USAAF fighters escorting heavy bombers targeting oil refineries. Spotting an Me 262 below his flight, Amoss dived on the jet and caught its pilot completely by surprise. His first burst struck the engines and the second, from just 200 yards astern of the fighter, caused

After the pair of jets bounced by Browning on 9 February sped out of range, he called Bochkay to say he would cover him as he pressed home his attack. That was the last anyone heard from Capt Browning. Two years after the war had ended, US Army officials spoke to two German civilians who witnessed what had happened to Browning. His Mustang was seen to collide with the Me 262 flown by Oberstleutnant Volprecht Freiherr von Riedesel, commander of KG(J) 54, and both aircraft spun to earth, crashing just 600 yards apart. With no recoverable remains, Capt James W Browning is listed on 'The Wall of the Missing' at the American Military Cemetery in Luxembourg (*Lt Col Clarence 'Bud' Anderson*)

Among Eighth Air Force fighter groups, the 55th FG was a relative latecomer in scoring jet victories. The first pilot to make a claim from the unit was 1Lt Walter J Konantz on 13 January 1945 – it was his second of three victories. On 15 February, 2Lt Dudley M Amoss was patrolling at low-altitude in this P-51D-5 (44-13818) when he bounced an Me 262 near Amberg and shot it down in flames. The pilot of the jet survived, bailing out of the burning jet at less than 500 ft (*55th FG Association*)

When Amoss claimed his Me 262 over Amberg, it brought his score to 2.5 victories. On 21 March 1945, he 'made ace' when he shot down three Fw 190s southwest of Münster. On the same mission he was hit by flak strafing Hopsten airfield, crash-landing in Holland and being taken prisoner (*55th FG Association*)

it to explode. Despite this, somehow the pilot still managed to bail out. On 21 March, Amoss 'made ace' by destroying three Fw 190s, only to be shot down by flak near Hopsten airfield minutes later. He spent the rest of the war as a PoW.

On 22 February the Allies launched more than 3000 aircraft from the RAF and the USAAF's Eighth, Ninth and Fifteenth Air Forces on Operation *Clarion*, which was the codename given to the systematic destruction of the German rail and road transportation network. In response to this aerial onslaught, JG 7 scrambled nearly 50 Me 262s, and they drew first blood shortly before 1200 hrs when ace Oberfeldwebel Hermann Buchner and future ace Oberfähnrich Heinz Russel of 3. *Staffel* prepared to attack 1st Air Division B-17s over Stendal. Just as they were about to intercept the bombers, the German pilots spotted formations of P-51s from the 352nd, 353rd and 364th FGs as they rendezvoused with the B-17s. Switching their focus to the fighters, Buchner and Russel bounced a section of Mustangs from the 364th FG out of the sun, the former sending the P-51 of 2Lt Francis X Radley down in flames for his 48th victory (of 52).

Elsewhere, other elements of the 353rd FG were on a freelance patrol in the area between Brandenburg and Moritz when a call came over the radio that bombers had reported jet aircraft in the vicinity of Brandenburg. 350th FS CO Maj Wayne K Blickenstaff was leading the group, and upon arriving in the area he spotted four Me 262s in a diving left turn. Three of the jets scattered, but one kept turning to the left. Blickenstaff pursued the latter through cloud, and when they broke out at 7000 ft he was directly over central Berlin. While still chasing the jet, he noticed another Me 262 heading in his direction some 3000 ft below him. Blickenstaff jettisoned his drop tanks, split-essed and set off after the second jet fighter.

When Blickenstaff had initially called out the four Me 262s, Capt Gordon B Compton was leading the 351st FS slightly above and to the left of the 350th FS. He began to pursue the third jet in the formation, but when he could not close the distance he turned his attention to another aircraft and waited for its pilot to pull out of his dive. When he did so, Compton was waiting;

'He turned right in front of me. I did not have time to track and range with my K-14 gunsight, so I picked out his line of flight and fired a long burst for him to fly through. I saw a few strikes on the right jet unit and it began leaving a trail of white smoke. With this unit crippled, the Me 262 was unable to pull away, and I got dead astern of him at a distance of about 350 yards. Pieces came off following one burst, and finally he pulled up sharply to the left, climbing several thousand feet per minute. Then the right jet unit burst into flames and the pilot rolled over and bailed out.'

Compton had just destroyed the first of two Me 262s that he would be credited with.

Meanwhile, back over Berlin, Blickenstaff pulled out of his split-S and tried to reacquire the Me 262 that had flown past him, but the German pilot had disappeared into low altitude haze that blanketed the area and escaped. After an eight-minute easterly pursuit Blickenstaff believed he was nearing the Soviet frontline, so he broke off and turned his flight back in the direction of home. As he passed through 8000 ft northwest of Berlin, Blickenstaff observed another Me 262 flying east through the haze. Once again, he rolled over in pursuit;

'I was able to pick up enough speed in the dive to close on this enemy aircraft, and I opened fire at a range of 600 to 700 yards. Strikes were observed in the left jet and a thin stream of smoke began to trail from it. Finding that I was able to close even more, I opened fire again at a range of 400-500 yards. The enemy pilot responded with some rather wild evasive action so that I was unable to keep my sight upon him. The Hun dove for the deck and started pulling away, but I scored strikes again on the left jet. Smoke began to pour out of the left jet. The pilot jettisoned the canopy and bailed out the right side. The plane rolled over to the left and split-essed into a forest.'

Blickenstaff's persistence had been rewarded, the Me 262 taking his tally to exactly five victories. He would claim three Fw 190s and two Bf 109s on 24 March, taking his final score to ten.

I. and II./KG(J) 54 took a beating again during the morning of 25 February, with 16 Me 262s being caught in the process of taking off from Gibelestadt by the 38th FS/55th FG. The unit was performing a fighter sweep in the Nurnberg area at 13,000 ft at the time, the jets being spotted by Capt Donald E Penn in the lead Mustang. He called for his flight to jettison their tanks, before engaging the Me 262s and in a swirling low-level dogfight that saw Penn and five other pilots from the 38th claim seven jets destroyed without loss.

Two of the Me 262s fell to Capt Donald M Cummings, who pursued one that broke left and down, allowing him to cut inside the jet's turn and shoot it down. Cummings and his wingman then climbed up to 5000 ft in search of other targets. He soon spotted an

On 22 February 1945, the Allies launched a sortie of more than 3000 aircraft against the Reich as part of Operation *Clarion*. The 353rd FG was on a freelance patrol that day when Maj Wayne K Blickenstaff chased an Me 262 that escaped, although he soon spotted a second over Berlin and chased it eastward towards Soviet lines before breaking off. He then found a third jet northwest of Berlin and shot it down at low level. This was Blickenstaff's fifth victory. On 24 March, now-Lt Col Blickenstaff became an 'ace in a day' when he shot down two Bf 109s and three Fw 190s (*Peter Randall collection*)

While on a fighter sweep near Nurnberg on 25 February 1945, the 55th FG clashed with 16 Me 262s from I. and II./KG(J) 54. In a huge low-level dogfight six pilots from the 38th FS shot down seven Me 262s, two of which were credited to Capt Donald M Cummings. He claimed the first jet quite quickly, but he was forced to chase the second one around the pattern at Leipheim airfield until he finally scored multiple hits, sending the jet down in flames. This made Cummings the second, and last, USAAF pilot to down two jets in a single sortie. He 'made ace' on 7 April when he downed a pair of Bf 109s over Celle (*55th FG Association*)

unidentified aircraft near Leipheim airfield as it flew over the base at about 4000 ft. Cummings quickly identified the fighter as an Me 262, and he chased it around the airfield until he was in a position to get off a deflection shot. He scored hits all over the aircraft, which rolled over and crashed. With this victory Cummings became the second USAAF pilot, after Urban Drew, to shoot down two jets in a single mission. These were Cummings' third and fourth victories, and a month later he shared a Bf 109 victory with squadronmate 1Lt Roger B Mooers and then 'made ace' on 7 April when he downed two Bf 109s over Celle.

KG(J) 54's ranks had been decimated in just 16 days of combat, with a further four Me 262s having been destroyed in strafing attacks on Gibelestadt and two in accidents on 25 February. Veteran bomber pilot Major Hansgeorg Bätcher was subsequently appointed *Geschwaderkommodore* of what remained of KG(J) 54, which now had just 20 Me 262s left.

Just as the Gibelstadt action came to a close, 1Lts Richard E White and Eugene Murphy from the 385th FS/364th FG were 200 miles to the north, near Lake Steinhude, when they spotted an Ar 234 at 2000 ft. They duly shot it down in an engagement that saw all three aircraft flying as low as just 30 ft! Although neither pilot would 'make ace', this victory was historically significant in that the 364th FG became the first group to score a victory against each of Germany's three jet aircraft – the Me 163, Me 262 and Ar 234. Only one other group would accomplish that feat, but not until the very end of the war.

While the *Clarion* battles raged in the skies over the increasingly beleaguered Third Reich, a new elite Me 262 unit had been established that would soon make its combat debut under the command of the Luftwaffe's most revered fighter pilot, General Adolf Galland. Designated *Jagdverband* (JV) 44, it would become known as *'Der Galland Zirkus'* ('The Galland Circus'). In terms of aerial victories, the *Jagdflieger* that served with JV 44 were amongst the most successful, and highly decorated, fighter pilots in the history of military aviation. Indeed, 17 of them had been awarded the Knight's Cross and the top five aces had a combined score of 934 victories.

On 1/2 March USAAF fighter pilots claimed six Me 262s shot down, although three are listed as unconfirmed. All three of the confirmed victories fell to non-aces, with one of them being claimed by 1Lt John K Wilkins of the 2nd Scouting Force. Three such units had been created in September 1944 to check for flak sites and Luftwaffe airfields, and gauge weather conditions, en route to target areas in advance of the heavy bombers. Scouting Force pilots (in P-51s) would be credited with downing three Me 262s by war's end. Another successful pilot on 2/3 March was 1Lt Theodore W Sedvert of the 353rd FS/354th FG, who subsequently claimed another Me 262 destroyed three weeks later, although its demise was unconfirmed.

As the Allies continued their advance eastward toward the River Rhine, Hitler ordered the destruction of all bridges over this last natural defence. On 7 March the Allies seized the final still-intact crossing – the soon-to-be-famous Ludendorff Bridge at Remagen. The Germans had set demolition charges on it and then detonated them, but the bridge still stood.

Reichsmarschall Herman Göring immediately made the bridge at Remagen the Luftwaffe's number one target. For the first week low clouds hampered attacks by Stukas and Fw 190 fighter-bombers, which were further frustrated by American anti-aircraft guns. On 7 March, a trio of Ar 234Bs from KG 76 attacked the bridge, but failed to inflict any damage. One bomber was shot down by American flak guns.

KG 76 was one of the oldest and most prestigious units in the Luftwaffe. The day after the Normandy landings, the Ju 88-equipped *Kampfgeschwader* was withdrawn from combat operations and became the first group to convert to the Ar 234. In mid-December 9./KG 76, under the command of Hauptmann Dieter Lukesch, became the first unit to be declared operational with 12 Ar 234B-2s. On Christmas Eve, the unit flew its first mission when eight aircraft bombed the city of Liège, in Belgium, in support of the Ardennes campaign.

On 11 March two more Arados made a visual bombing run on the bridge, but again they failed to score any hits. On the 12th and 13th, KG 76 flew 37 sorties against the bridge, but the method of attack employed by the Ar 234 pilots had been changed. These attacks were carried out using the Egon radar-operated aiming system, and level bombing runs were made at between 16,000 ft and 26,000 ft. Nevertheless, the bridge at Remagen still stood.

So far, KG 76 had only lost a single aircraft to enemy action (flak) during its sustained campaign against the Ludendorff Bridge, but this all changed on 14 March. High-scoring ace Capt Donald Bryan of the 328th FS/352nd FG had encountered Ar 234s on three separate occasions, but had only managed to claim one as damaged, on 21 December. On 14 March he was leading a flight of P-51s that was escorting Ninth Air Force A-26 Invaders, Bryan flying 1Lt George A Middleton's P-51K 44-11628 *WORRA BIRD 3/BASHFUL BETSY* near Remagen when the Ar 234 flown by Hauptmann Hirschberger of 6./KG 76 was spotted passing beneath his flight;

'I dropped my tanks and started after the enemy aircraft. He was travelling about 50 mph faster than we were and crossed the Rhine south of the bridge, going west, then turned north and made a very shallow diving run on the bridge, but he did not drop his bombs. I saw several P-47s to the northwest, so I headed in a northeasterly direction. I could not catch the enemy aircraft in a straight run, and thought he might turn east to avoid combat with the P-47s.'

Bryan's assumption that the Arado pilot would attempt to avoid the Thunderbolts was correct, and Hirschberger passed under Bryan again;

Once the Allies crossed Ludendorff Bridge over the River Rhine River on 7 March 1945, Reichsmarschall Hermann Göring made the bridge at Remagen the Luftwaffe's number one target. For days the Ar 234Bs of KG 76 flew dozens of sorties against the bridge, but failed to destroy it. On 14 March double ace Capt Donald S Bryan of the 328th FS/352nd FG chased an Ar 234 with dogged determination until he hit its right engine, but Hauptmann Hirschberger of 6./KG 76 continued to take evasive action. Bryan finally hit the second engine and the bomber crashed near Elsaffthal. The Ar 234 was Bryan's final victory of the war, taking his tally to 13.333 kills (*352nd FG Association*)

'When he passed under me I dove down on him and opened fire at about 250 yards. I hit him with the first burst and apparently knocked out his right jet engine. He made a shallow turn to the right and started mild evasive manoeuvres. They consisted of shallow turns and a few shallow dives and climbs.'

In an interview with artist Troy White, Bryan explained that he had fired almost all of his ammunition and knocked out both of the Ar 234's engines. He then noticed several of his squadronmates and a similar number of P-47s lining up for a shot at the ailing bomber, but Bryan was having none of it. Unlike the previous three Ar 234s he had engaged, this one was not going to get away. Bryan's Encounter Report continued;

'The enemy aircraft was emitting much white smoke but I don't believe it caught fire. At about the time I finished firing he rolled over on his back and dived straight into the ground and exploded. Just before hitting the ground the pilot jettisoned his canopy, but did not get out.'

The Ar 234 proved to be Bryan's final victory of the war, his tally of 13.333 aerial victories making him the second-highest scorer in the 328th FS.

Later that afternoon 1Lt Robert E Barnhart was leading 'Vortex Blue' Flight from the 360th FS/356th FG, which was covering the last formation of bombers coming off targets in Hildesheim. About ten minutes after departing from the target area the Allied ground-control radar station codenamed 'Nuthouse' reported bandits near Hildesheim. Barnhart took his flight of Mustangs back to the target area, but no enemy aircraft were spotted. After ten minutes of fruitless searching he turned westward, at which point Barnhart spotted a bandit at his altitude on a reciprocal course. He banked around behind the aeroplane and set off after it in an easterly direction, but after 15 minutes of full-throttle pursuit Barnhart's fuel status forced him to break off the chase and head in the direction of home.

Moments later, the aircraft he had been pursuing – which Barnhart had still not identified – turned north, allowing the P-51 pilot to cut him off and close the distance. It was obvious to Barnhart that the bandit was unaware of 'Vortex Blue's' presence. His Encounter Report detailed what happened next;

'Unable to identify it, I closed until I saw the open jets and German markings. Knowing that I had him cold, I slid under him and came up on his right, about 30 ft from his right plane. I could not identify it then, but have since recognised it from drawings as an Arado 234. The pilot of the jet looked over at me and immediately jettisoned his canopy and bailed out.'

Despite now being pilotless, the bomber maintained its altitude and right hand orbit, allowing Barnhart to make a series of gun camera passes – he also filmed the pilot hanging beneath his parachute. Figuring the jet would eventually crash, Barnhart

When Capt Bryan shot down the Ar 234 over Remagen on 14 March 1945 he was not flying his assigned P-51D-10 44-14061 *Little One III*, but P-51K-5 44-11628 *BASHFUL BETSY*, normally flown by Capt George A Middleton. This Mustang was unusual in that is carried two names. On the left side it was christened *WORRA BIRD 3* (the name given to it by Middleton) and on the right side crew chief Sgt Joe Shenk applied the name *BASHFUL BETSY* (*352nd FG Association*)

reformed his flight, but as he looked back the Ar 234 was still in its orbit. He returned to the jet, made several more gun camera passes and then opened fire, sending the Arado down a vertical dive until it hit the ground. Barnhart later noted that the jet 'exploded violently'. The Ar 234 was Barnhart's second of two aerial victories.

The following day (15 March), the USAAF claimed its final Me 163 victory. Since Capt Arthur Jeffrey had downed the first Komet to fall to the Allies on 29 July 1944, USAAF fighters had destroyed an additional four rocket fighters, with the most recent pair falling to the guns of 4th FG aces Freddie Glover and Louis Norley on 2 November. On 15 March, the only USAAF pilot to engage a jet was ranking 359th FG ace Capt Ray S Wetmore of the 370th FS, who was leading 'Red' Section near Wittenberg in P-51D 44-15521 *SCREAMIN DEMON*. Flying at 25,000 ft with a formation of heavy bombers, Wetmore spotted a pair of Me 163s circling at 20,000 ft and promptly dived on the rocket fighters. As he closed to within 3000 yards, one of the Komet pilots spotted the incoming Mustangs and lit his motor, pulling into a 70-degree climb. Wetmore later noted in his Encounter Report;

Although he was not an ace, 1Lt Robert E Barnhart of the 356th FG had an unusual encounter with an Ar 234 on 14 March. After pursuing the Arado eastward for nearly 15 minutes, the jet turned, which allowed Barnhart to close the distance. He approached unseen from below and joined up in formation off the jet's right wing. Upon looking over and seeing the Mustang, the pilot bailed out without Barnhart firing a shot. When the Arado continued to fly by itself, Barnhart decided to shoot it down (*Peter Randall collection*)

'At about 26,000 ft his jet quit, so he split-essed. I dived with him and levelled off at 2000 ft on him at "six o'clock". During the dive my IAS [indicated air speed] was between 550-600 mph. I opened fire at 200 yards. Pieces flew off all over. He made a sharp turn to the right and I gave him another short burst, and half his left wing flew off and the plane caught fire. The pilot bailed out, and I watched the enemy aircraft crash into the ground.'

Flt Off Russel E Shouse was flying as 'Red 3', and having witnessed Wetmore's engagement he wrote in his confirmation report that the enemy pilot bailed out at just 500 ft. Even with available German records, the identity of the Komet and its pilot remain a mystery. As previously noted, this Me 163 was the last example to be shot down by the USAAF, and it was also Capt Wetmore's final victory, taking his tally to 21.25 aerial and 2.333 strafing victories. He was the fifth-ranking USAAF ace in the ETO.

Both Me 262s and Ar 234s were active once again on 19 March, with two Arado bombers falling to three non-aces from the 82nd FS/78th FG who had all previously made claims against jets. A short while later, 200 miles southeast of where the 78th had downed the Ar 234s, the 359th FG was patrolling south of Dessau. Leading the 368th FS in P-51D 44-15717 *WILD BILL* was unit CO, Maj Niven K Cranfill, who had so far shot down four enemy aircraft, including three fighters during a single mission on 27 November 1944. While patrolling at 18,000 ft, Cranfill spotted three Me 262s passing overhead. The Mustang pilots jettisoned their tanks and started to climb in pursuit. Shortly thereafter Cranfill saw ten more jets fly beneath the squadron in a southerly direction. He immediately broke off the pursuit of the trio above him and went after the larger formation. The Mustang pilots were unable to close the distance on the jets, however, and Cranfill watched helplessly as they attacked a box formation of B-17s.

One of the jets then made a 180-degree turn that put Cranfill in a position to bounce the Me 262, as his Encounter Report explained;

'I saw one ME 262 on the tail of a P-51 and bounced him. He broke off when I fired several bursts from line astern, getting strikes in the wings. I claimed this one damaged. I followed him north and saw he was passing another 262. I opened [the throttle] wide open, indicating 380 [mph] straight and level at 12,000 ft, and was able to close on the latter. I started shooting from astern, a little below, 600 to 800 yards, and got good strikes on the bottom of the fuselage. The enemy aircraft then started a diving turn to the left, from which he did not recover.'

As Cranfill levelled off at 5000 ft he saw another Mustang make a pass at the jet, but failed to get any hits. The Me 262 crashed in a vertical attitude and exploded. After review Maj Cranfill was awarded full credit for destroying one Me 262 and damaging another, thus finishing the war as a five-victory ace.

After claiming just 2.5 jet victories in 1944, the 357th FG had racked up six victories in three engagements in January and February 1945. On 19 March ace Maj Robert W Foy and Capt Robert S Fifield of the 363rd FS added to that score whilst on an escort mission to the Ruhland, with ace Lt Col Andrew Evans leading the group. Just after 1400 hrs, the 357th witnessed the largest concentration of jet fighters yet seen – 36 – attack the bombers near Chemnitz. The Me 262s came in from 'six o'clock high' in nine flights of four, with the final two flights approaching at a slower speed than the rest. Ace Lt Col Tommy Hayes, who was leading the 363rd FS, broke into the last two flights. The jets broke away from the bombers and split up into two-ship elements, which easily out-ran the Mustangs. By breaking up the last two flights, Hayes had certainly saved some bombers, for the third flight of jets had succeeded in shooting down four B-17s – single aircraft from the 96th and 385th BGs and two from the 452nd BG. There were 40 men aboard the four Flying Fortresses, but only 19 parachutes were seen.

1Lt Ray Wetmore of the 370th FS/359th FG scored his first aerial victory on 10 February 1944, 'made ace' on 19 May, double ace (as a captain) on 2 November, triple ace on 1 January 1945 and quadruple ace and 'ace in a day' on 14 January. He scored his final victory, an Me 163, on 15 March 1945. Wetmore finished the war as the fifth highest scoring ace in the ETO with 21.25 victories, 17 of which were claimed in the Mustang (*359th FG Association*)

Capt Ray Wetmore's P-51D-10 44-14733 *Daddy's Girl* (seen here at East Wretham) is well-known, but when he shot down his Me 163 on 15 March 1945 he was flying P-51D-15 44-15521 *SCREAMIN DEMON*. Wetmore followed the Komet into a split-s manoeuvre at 26,000 ft and pushed his Mustang to nearly 600 mph in a dive, before levelling out at 2000 ft. He then fired several bursts from 200 yards astern that blew the Komet's left wing off. The pilot bailed out and the fighter spun in and exploded (*359th FG Association*)

While Lt Col Hayes was doing his best to disrupt this devastating attack, Capt Robert S Fifield demonstrated incredible tenacity in his encounter with one of the Me 262s;

'I was leading the second element of "Cement Blue" Flight when 20+ 262s attacked our box from "six o'clock, slightly high". I dropped my tanks and tried to beat them to the bombers. I got there just as they hit. I shot at about four different ones and finally singled one out. They were all diving to the left. They were getting away from me, so I tried lobbing some long-range shots in and finally got some black smoke trailing from one of them. After that he slowed down and I started closing in on him. They seemed to split into elements of two. After I got some more hits, his wingman got up close to him and then took off again when I got some more hits. I closed up to about 400 yards and got many hits. He trailed some smoke and then went straight in and exploded.'

During this action, 1Lt Joe Cannon got his one and only shot at becoming a 'jet killer'. When he spotted the Me 262s coming in on the bombers, he broke into them and latched on to the tail of one of the jets, closing to within 200 yards. Cannon fired a short burst and saw strikes on the tail, at which point the light bulb illuminating his K-14 gunsight blew out. After firing several more bursts, without effect, the Me 262 broke left and dived out of range, leaving Cannon with a mere 'damaged' claim.

Shortly thereafter, in the vicinity of Giessen, Maj Foy spotted three Me 262s closing in on a flight of Mustangs. Leading his own flight down in an attempt to intercept the enemy jets, he set his sights on the Me 262 on the left side of the formation. Spotting the P-51s closing on them from the rear, the German pilots began to accelerate out of range. Foy, however, used his K-14 gunsight to good effect by hitting the left engine of his quarry with a well-placed burst. The fighter, trailing smoke, rolled over into a split-s and crashed near an airfield. This success took Maj Foy's tally of aerial victories to 14, and he claimed his 15th and final victory five days later.

The fact that the vast majority of jet victories were scored by pilots with less than five kills was highlighted over the next three days (20-22 March), when 13 Me 262s were shot down by 12 non-aces, four of whom were multiple jet killers, from the 55th, 78th, 339th and 361st FGs. The highest scoring non-ace in this group was 1Lt John A Kirk of the 83rd FS/78th FG, whose Me 262 on 21 March near Meiningen was the last of his four aerial victories – he also claimed six strafing kills. The sole ace to make a claim during this 72-hour period of intense action was Capt William J Dillard of the Italy-based 308th FS/31st FG. Escorting Fifteenth Air Force bombers over the Ruhland area, his Me 262 victory on the 22nd gave him ace status. He would claim a Bf 110 destroyed southeast of Prague three days later for his last kill.

On 24 March the Allies launched a massive airborne assault on the eastern side of the River Rhine, codenamed Operation *Varsity*. Its objective

On 19 March 1945 eight USAAF pilots combined to shoot down two Ar 234s and four Me 262s, but only two of those pilots were, or became, aces. Amongst the latter was Maj Niven K Cranfill, CO of the 359th FG's 368th FS. He scored his first victory on 16 August 1944 and added three more on 27 November. On 19 March Cranfill initially damaged an Me 262 that was chasing another Mustang. Minutes later he bounced a second Me 262 and fired a burst from 800 yards that sent the Me 262 into a diving left turn from which it did not recover. This was Cranfill's fifth, and final, victory of the war (*359th FG Association*)

When Maj Cranfill claimed his 'ace-making' victory over an Me 262 on 19 March he was flying P-51D-15 44-15717, which is seen here in this rare aerial shot of a flight of 359th FG Mustangs on a bomber escort mission near war's end. This aircraft was later assigned to Cranfill's replacement as CO of the 368th FS, Lt Col James W Parsons, who named it *WILD WILL* (*Peter Randall collection*)

Maj Robert W Foy of the 363rd FS/357th FS also claimed a jet victory on 19 March when he used his K-14 gunsight to fire an effective long-range burst that struck the left engine of an Me 262, which then rolled over and crashed near an airfield. This was Foy's only jet victory, although he had claimed another Me 262 damaged on 9 February. Foy finished the war with 15 confirmed aerial victories (© *IWM FRE 3111*)

was to assist Field Marshal Bernard Montgomery's 21st Army Group in securing footholds along both sides of the Rhine. In order to draw pressure off the *Varsity* offensive, the Fifteenth Air Force launched its longest mission of the war – a 1600-mile round trip to the Daimler-Benz engine plant in the heart of Berlin.

Among the fighter pilots tasked with escorting Fifth Bomb Wing B-17s that day were the Tuskegee Airmen of the 332nd FG. The latter duly relieved the P-38-equipped 1st FG over Kaaden, then in southern Germany and now part of the Czech Republic. When the 31st FG was subsequently late relieving the 332nd, the Tuskegee Airmen were forced to continue flying their P-51s on to Berlin. As the bombers neared the German capital at 1208 hrs, they were attacked by 15 Me 262s from Parchim-based 9. and 10./JG 7, thus signalling the start of a ten-minute dogfight that eventually ended with eight jets destroyed by the Mustang pilots of the 31st and 332nd FGs. Amongst the trio of successful pilots from the latter unit was 1Lt Roscoe Brown, who was leading the 100th FS on this occasion. Stephen Chapis interviewed Dr Brown in 2013;

'We saw the jets about five minutes prior to the target, and the engagement lasted about ten minutes. I was about 500 ft below the bombers when they were attacked. We tried to catch the jets as they were climbing up. I was leading the entire squadron – 16 airplanes – and was the first one to identify the jets. I said "Drop your tanks and follow me". We made a hard turn to the right and I got on the tail of one of the Me 262s – in his blind spot. He was climbing, and failed to see me. I got the K-14 circle on him and held it there as I pulled the trigger, and he blew up.'

The pilot of the Me 262, ten-victory ace *Staffelführer* Oberleutnant Franz Külp of 10./JG 7, was so severely injured when he bailed out of his burning jet that he was still hospitalised at war's end. Moments prior to being shot down, Külp had claimed a B-24 destroyed.

Just as the Tuskegee pilots disengaged, the 31st FG, led by group CO Col William A Daniel, finally arrived on the scene. Daniel stated the following in his Encounter Report;

'At 1225 hrs, from 28,000 ft just south of the target, I observed two Me 262s headed towards the bombers from "eleven o'clock". The bombers were headed north, the enemy fighters were headed east and I was headed west, putting me 180 degrees from the enemy aircraft and 90 degrees to the bombers. As I saw the two enemy aircraft turn into the bombers from astern, I turned in and started to close and fire. However, I then observed four more enemy aircraft turning in. I waited for the No 6 enemy aircraft to turn in, then closed in on him from about "4.30 o'clock" to 500 yards and fired. No strikes were observed, although the enemy aircraft snap-rolled and went into a spin. I observed a parachute and four blobs of smoke.'

This Me 262 was Col Daniel's fifth, and last, aerial victory.

For all the 24 March victors, with the exception of Col Daniel, these Me 262 kills were their only victories of the war, and the last that the 31st FG would score against the jets.

1Lt Roscoe Brown watches Sgt Marcellus Smith working on the Packard V-1650-7 fitted in his P-51D at Ramitelli airfield, in Italy, in the spring of 1945. Brown was one of three Tuskegee Airmen from the 332nd FG to down Me 262s on 24 March 1945 during the group's marathon 1600-mile escort mission to Berlin (*NARA*)

On 25 March, all three air divisions of the Eighth Air Force were tasked with hitting German oil refineries, but only the B-24s – 243 of them to be exact – from the 2nd Air Division were able to reach their targets. The Liberators were escorted by Mustangs and Thunderbolts from the 56th, 339th, 352nd, 361st and 479th FGs, which were met by Me 262s from both JG 7 and KG(J) 54. The jets wreaked havoc on the B-24s of the 448th BG in particular, with a formation leader being shot down just after reaching the Initial Point (when the aircraft was under the lateral control of the bombardier on the run in to the target). Two more were lost over the target itself and another was so badly damaged that the crew bailed out shortly after dropping their ordnance. An additional ten bombers received significant damage from the Me 262's quartet of hard-hitting MK 108 30 mm cannon.

As this carnage was erupting, the first fighters to arrive on the scene were from the 479th FG, including 1Lt Eugene H Wendt, who duly scored his fourth, and final, victory of the war when he shot down the Me 262 of Feldwebel Fritz Taube from 10./JG 7 shortly after he had himself destroyed a B-24.

When the jets first attacked the Liberators, Capt Raymond H Littge of the 487th FS/352nd FG, leading 'Yellow' Flight, had quickly latched on to an Me 262. After a 15-minute chase, he broke off the pursuit as they closed on Rechlin-Lärz airfield, near Müritz Lake, and loitered in the area in the hope of catching a jet in the landing pattern. He did not have to wait long, spotting Oberleutnant Schatzle, a former bomber pilot recently assigned to 9./JG 7, approaching the field. Littge's Encounter Report described what happened next;

'After I circled it [Rechlin-Lärz airfield] for five minutes, an Me 262 came over the field – presumably the same one I had chased before – and peeled off. As he was lowering his wheels I made a 100-degree pass at him, seeing no strikes. He levelled off then and I got behind him and fired several long bursts. I saw quite a few strikes, several of which set his right jet on fire. His evasive action consisted of gentle left and right turns.

When 243 Liberators hit oil refineries near Hitzacker on 25 March 1945, they were met by Me 262s from JG 7 and KG(J) 54. These aircraft duly shot down four bombers and damaged ten more. After a futile 15-minute chase in pursuit of a jet fighter, Capt Raymond H Littge of the 487th FS/352nd FG broke off and began circling the Me 262 airfield at Rechlin instead. Just five minutes later, the jet flown by Oberleutnant Schatzle attempted to land, and Littge set its right engine on fire. The pilot pulled up and bailed out, but his parachute did not open. This final victory made Littge a double ace (*352nd FG Association*)

He jettisoned his canopy, pulled up to 2000 ft and bailed out. His 'chute did not open.'

Schatzle's Me 262 took Littge's final tally to 10.5 victories – he also claimed 13 strafing kills.

The Thunderbolts of the 56th FG were part of the escort force that day, and 63rd FS CO Maj George E Bostwick was leading his flight in P-47M 44-21160 *"Devastatin Deb"*. The Thunderbolt pilots pursued a number of jets as they fled eastward towards their base a Parchim, where Bostwick lined up on an Me 262 that was on its final approach. Instead of landing, however, the jet continued flying down the runway and passed directly over another Me 262 that was taking off. Bostwick shifted his sights to the second aircraft and fired a burst just as the pilot broke left. Instead of turning out of Bostwick's fire, the pilot dug his jet's left wingtip into the ground, causing the fuel-laden Me 262 to cartwheel before exploding. Bostwick then turned his attention back to his original target, firing an ineffective burst from more than 800 yards as the jet sped out of range.

The jet fighter was Bostwick's sixth aerial victory, and he would claim two more kills on 7 April (as well as damaging another Me 262) to finish the war with eight – plus six strafing victories. During this same engagement on 25 March, 2Lt Edwin M Crosthwait Jnr, who was flying as Bostwick's No 4, scored his only victory of the war when he downed Oberfähnrich Günther Ullrich of 9./JG 7, who was flying Me 262A-1b Wk-Nr 110796. Ulrich had also claimed a B-24 destroyed just prior to his own demise, taking his tally to five victories.

On 30 March, the Eighth Air Force launched a massive raid on the U-boat pens and oil storage tanks in Hamburg, Bremen, Wilhelmshaven and Farge. More than 1300 bombers, escorted by nearly 900 fighters, participated in the operation, and JG 7 scrambled 30 jets to meet the raid. At 1330 hrs over Hamburg, Leutnant Kurt Schnörrer shot down two B-17s and one-armed 64-victory ace Leutnant Viktor Petermann claimed a probable. However, Schnörrer's fighter was hit by crossfire from the bombers' gunners, forcing him to bail out. As he left the cockpit Schnörrer struck the jet's tail, breaking his leg and putting him out of the war for the duration. Schnörrer was a Knight's Cross winner with 35 victories on the eastern front, and after he took command of 2./JG 7 he became a double jet ace with 11 kills, including nine four-engined bombers.

Over the next 30 minutes a number of clashes took place between the Me 262s of JG 7 and Mustangs from the 55th, 339th, 352nd, 361st and 364th FGs. The P-51 pilots claimed six jets destroyed (again, none of these aviators were aces) for the loss of a single Mustang, and its pilot, from the 339th.

Approximately 30 minutes after the main action over Hamburg, the 78th FG had just cleared the target area when the group was released to look for targets of opportunity. By this point in the war 14 pilots from 78th's 82nd and 83rd FSs had shot down ten Me 262s and two Ar 234s, with several falling to the guns of junior officers. Conspicuously absent from the jet victory list was the 84th FS. The group's CO and veteran ace Lt Col John D Landers led the 78th north towards Kiel, his wingman on this occasion being 2Lt Thomas V Thain Jnr from the 84th. The latter had a single Bf 109 to his credit. Just after 1400 hrs, as the prowling Mustangs neared Rendsberg at 7000 ft, Landers spotted an Me 262 down on the

Pilots from of all three squadrons within the 56th FG pose with one of their beloved Thunderbolts in June 1944. Known as 'Zemke's Wolfpack', the 56th was the only Eighth Air Force fighter group not to convert to the Mustang. During the war, nine pilots from the 56th shot down 5.5 Me 262s and 2.5 Ar 234s, although Maj George E Bostwick, seated fourth from the right, was the only 'Wolfpack' jet killer to 'make ace' (*Peter Randall collection*)

Maj George Bostwick was already a five-kill ace when he shot down an Me 262 that was taking off from Parchim on 25 March 1945 while flying P-47M-1 44-21160 *"Devastatin Deb"*. During the same engagement, Bostwick's No 4, 2Lt Edwin M Crosthwait Jnr, scored his only victory of the war when he shot down an Me 262 from 9./JG 7. Bostwick finished the war with eight victories (*Peter Randall collection*)

deck. As he bounced the jet, its pilot made a gentle left turn, and as Landers closed the distance the Me 262 completed a 180-degree turn to drag the Mustangs over the flak defences of Rendsburg airfield. As he flew through light and inaccurate flak, Landers fired a burst from 700 yards that struck one of the jet's engines. When the German pilot attempted another turn, Landers fired again from 400 yards;

'The ME 262 made a steep left bank and my next burst hit him in the cockpit area. As I overshot, the jet levelled out and started a gentle glide. My wingman, Lt Thain, pulled in behind, hit him solidly with a long burst and overshot. The enemy aircraft continued in this glide, then crashed and burned. The pilot did not get out.'

This shared kill was Landers' final aerial victory of the war. He had claimed 14.5 aerial and 20 strafing victories whilst flying with three fighter groups – one in the Pacific and two in the ETO. The Me 262 was also the final victory credited to 2Lt Thain, and the only jet downed by the 84th FS.

The following day (31 March) four more Me 262s were lost to USAAF fighters, one of which fell to future ace 1Lt Harrison B Tordoff of the 352nd FS/353rd FG over Dessau. He had claimed two aerial and two strafing successes in the P-47 in August-September 1944, after which his unit transitioned to the P-51. Tordoff would 'make ace' on 7 April, ending the conflict with five aerial and 4.5 strafing victories.

Two lesser-known units were also credited with single Me 262s on 31 March, namely the P-51-equipped 2nd Scouting Force (1Lt Marvin H Castleberry) and the Ninth Air Force's 406th FS/371st FG (Capt William T Bales Jnr), flying P-47s.

The final kill recorded on this date went to 1Lt Wayne L Coleman of the 82nd FS/78th FG. On 9 September 1944, then-2Lt Coleman had shot down three Fw 190s in his very first engagement. By 31 March, he been promoted and was now leading 'Surtax Red' Flight on an escort mission to Derben. At 1000 hrs, Coleman's flight, sweeping the target area at 15,000 ft ahead of the bombers, spotted two Me 262s flying on parallel course, but they flew out of range and disappeared. Coleman then saw another jet fighter and went in pursuit of it. After a lengthy chase, during which several flights fired on the Me 262 without effect, the jet disappeared into smoke and haze. Shortly thereafter, Coleman spotted it again at his 'low ten o'clock'. Performing a split-s manoeuvre, he rapidly closed in on the jet. 'I fired and observed a great many strikes on the canopy and right jet unit. The Me 262 pulled up slightly and I broke to the left. The jet did a roll to the right and went straight into the ground and exploded'. This was Coleman's fourth, and final, victory of the war.

CHAPTER FIVE

TO THE DEATH

As the Allies on the western front pushed farther into Germany, they overran many of the Luftwaffe's jet bases. KG(J) 51 was forced to move east to airfields in Bavaria, namely Munich-Riem, Fürth and Memmingen. General Galland also moved JV 44 to Munich-Riem, while 1./JG 7 departed Kaltenkirchen for Briest, Burg and Oranienburg, over which several intense dogfights would be fought in this final full month of the war in Europe.

The first of these occurred on 4 April, when the Eighth Air Force launched all of its fighter groups and all but one bomb group against airfields across northern Germany, the final bomb group hitting the U-boat pens in Hamburg. The latter mission would elicit the largest response yet from the Me 262s, with close to 50 jets armed with fearsome R4M aerial rockets being sortied. Over the course of an hour they fought a series of simultaneous running battles with Mustangs from the 4th, 339th and 364th FGs of the Eighth Air Force and Thunderbolts from the 1st Tactical Air Force's 324th FG, during which nine Me 262s and a single Ar 234 were shot down. The victors from the 324th, all from the 316th FS, were 1Lts Andrew Kandis and John W Haun, who each downed an Me 262, and 1Lt Mortimer J Thompson, who shot down the Arado. These were the only jet victories scored by the 324th FG during World War 2.

On this day, 383rd FS CO Lt Col George F Ceuleers was leading A Group of the 364th FG that was escorting B-17s to the Hamburg

On 4 April 1945, Lt Col George F Ceuleers, CO of the 364th FG's 383rd FS, chased an Me 262 for more than 20 minutes in this P-51D-25 (44-72719) before scoring a number of hits. The jet suddenly pitched up and the pilot bailed out and went right over Ceuleers' left wing. This final victory for Lt Col Ceuleers took his score to 10.5 aerial victories (*Peter Randall collection*)

JG 7 had claimed nine bombers and three fighters destroyed on 4 April 1945, and the following day JG 7 was credited with the destruction of six more USAAF heavy bombers for the loss of just one Me 262. The latter was claimed by Capt John C Fahringer of the 63rd FS/56th FG, this victory – his fourth and final – being scored at the controls of P-47M-1 44-21160 *"Devastatin Deb"*. This was the same Thunderbolt that Maj George E Bostwick had been flying when he scored a solitary Me 262 victory on 25 March (*Peter Randall collection*)

U-boat pens. On his way back to England, Ceuleers spotted a formation of B-24s heading into Germany that were under attack from enemy fighters. He and his flight had a height advantage over the German aircraft, which turned out to be eight Me 262s, and the Mustang pilot pushed the power up to 3000 rpm and 60 inches of manifold pressure before diving after the jets. Ceuleers quickly latched on to an Me 262 and chased it for nearly 20 minutes. Finally, he closed to within 500 yards and fired a few bursts, before firing again at a distance of just 100 yards. This time he saw his rounds hitting home, shortly after which the jet pitched up and the pilot jettisoned the canopy and bailed out, sailing right over Ceuleers' left wing. The victory proved to be Ceuleers' last, taking his tally to 10.5 aerial victories (1.5 of them scored in the P-38).

It had been a costly day of combat over Germany for both sides, for although JG 7 had suffered substantial losses to USAAF P-47s and P-51s, the Me 262 pilots had claimed eight Flying Fortresses, two Mustangs, a Liberator and a Thunderbolt destroyed.

There were far fewer Me 262 sorties flown on 5 April, but the few jets that were up again wreaked havoc on the heavy bombers – no fewer than six B-17s and B-24s were shot down for the loss of just one Me 262 in aerial combat. That morning 53 Thunderbolts of the 56th FG were escorting formations of B-17s to Regensburg when a solitary Me 262 made a pass from 'three o'clock' to 'nine o'clock' and shot down a Flying Fortress from the 401st BG. The pilot then started a right turn almost immediately in front of 'Blue' Flight of the 63rd FS, led by the unit's Operations Officer, Capt John C Fahringer, in P-47M 44-21160 *"Devastatin Deb"* – the same Thunderbolt used by Maj George E Bostwick to shoot down an Me 262 on 25 March.

The P-47 pilots jettisoned their tanks and headed down in pursuit. 1Lt Phillip Kuhn fired first, before overshooting, after which Fahringer rolled in on the Me 262's tail and let it have several bursts to no effect. However, the German pilot then made the fatal mistake of tightening his turn, which allowed Fahringer to close in to lethal range. At 500 yards, he opened up again with his Thunderbolt's eight 0.50-cal machine guns, and as the smoke began pouring from the jet Fahringer saw something go down the right side of his P-47. It was the pilot of the Me 262. The jet's demise gave Capt Fahringer his fourth victory, and, frustratingly for him, he would not have the opportunity to 'make ace' before war's end.

A force of nearly 1300 bombers was launched against the jet airfields and marshalling yards in northern and central Germany on 7 April, and although it had been badly battered three days prior, III./JG 7 launched 44 Me 262s and I./KG(J) 54 put up 15 jets. The 479th FG was one of the fighter groups assigned to protect the B-17s and B-24s, its pilots being tasked with escorting bombers to the Duneberg area. 2Lt Hilton O Thompson of the 434th FS was flying as 'Newcross Purple Three', his squadron being positioned high and to the left of the lead box of bombers and 'Newcross Purple' Flight protecting the northernmost side of the formation farthest away from the lead bombers.

At 1220 hrs Thompson saw six Me 262s, flying in three elements, coming in from 'nine o'clock' and heading for the bombers. He attempted to engage the jets but they were quickly out of range. Somehow, Thompson then became separated from his flight and found himself alone over central Germany. As he searched for his squadron at 26,000 ft, he spotted a lone Me 262 in a gentle climbing left turn about 2000 ft above him. Thompson also began climbing in pursuit of the jet, his Encounter Report describing the high altitude action that subsequently transpired;

'By cutting inside his turn I closed to within about 800 yards after having chased him up to 31,000 ft. Upon firing two short bursts I saw a few strikes on the left wing of the Me 262, and at the same time he increased his turn to the left, finally rolled over and went straight down. I fired several bursts during this time and saw many hits on and around the cockpit. After following him down about 5000 ft I saw large pieces fly from his aircraft, so I pulled out of my dive since my speed was becoming very high. I did not see that Me 262 again.'

After 2Lt Thompson fired his last burst he saw three or four other 'Newcross' Mustangs below him chasing the same jet. Nevertheless, he was awarded a full credit for destroying the Me 262 with 596 rounds of armour-piercing incendiaries.

Whilst 2Lt Thompson and the rest of 'Newcross Purple' Flight went after the first six Me 262s to target the bombers from the northern side of the formation, the 479th FG's 435th FS (covering the rear of the formation), including Capt Verne E Hooker, engaged a pair of jets that attacked the bombers from 'seven o'clock low'. In two brief but deadly dogfights Hooker claimed his only two aerial victories (he also had four strafing kills) of the war – a Bf 109 and an Me 262.

Despite not officially destroying a jet on 7 April, the most successful 479th pilot to emerge from this mission was the 434th FS's 1Lt Richard G Candelaria, who engaged a pair of Me 262s that were making head-on passes through a formation of Liberators southwest of Lüneburg. His Encounter Report read in part;

'I came at the leader head-on, trying to make him break, but he avoided my head-on pass by diving, and not altering his course, making it very difficult for me to hit him. I tried to drop my tanks on him, but missed completely. I half-rolled and lined-up on his tail as he opened fire on the bombers. I opened fire on the jet, observing hits on both sides of his cockpit and wings, then large puffs of smoke spat from the fuselage and wings.

'In the meantime, the second jet had positioned himself on my tail and opened fire on me. I saw white and red shells, like golf balls, going past me. Looking up into the rearview mirror, I saw him firing away. A moment later, he hit me in the right wing. Then, the first jet I had engaged broke away to the left in a lazy half-roll and went straight down, trailing smoke. I broke hard into the jet behind me, but he went off in a shallow dive towards his buddy, going much too fast for me to ever hope to catch.'

Candelaria was only awarded a probable, despite flight-mate 1Lt Floyd W Salze reporting that the jet rolled over into a dive from 17,000 ft and was still in the dive when it entered the clouds at 2500 ft, making it unlikely that the pilot recovered in time. Later in the mission Candelaria shot down four Bf 109s, and these victories, when combined with the two Fw 190s he destroyed on 5 December 1944, gave him a final tally of six aerial kills. On 13 April Candelaria's Mustang was hit by 20 mm and 40 mm flak while strafing the airfield at Rostock, and although wounded in the head and left arm, he managed to bail out of his stricken fighter. He evaded detection for ten days before being captured, thus spending the final weeks of the war as a PoW.

Only a handful of Me 262s were encountered on 8 and 9 April, resulting in just three victory claims being made by USAAF pilots. The solitary kill on the 8th fell to 1Lt John J Usiatynski of the 367th FS/358th FG, this proving to be the only confirmed jet victory credited to this Thunderbolt-equipped group from the Ninth Air Force. 1Lt Leo D Volkmer of the group's 365th FS claimed a Me 262 probable later in the month.

On the 9th the 361st FG was credited with its final Me 262 victory when 374th FS pilot 2Lt James T Sloan, flying P-51D 44-15323, shot one jet down and damaged a second while escorting bombers of the 2nd Air Division that were targeting airfields known to be used by the aircraft. Five days earlier, pilots from the group had escorted B-24s from this division to Parchim airfield, the bombers being attacked several times by defending Me 262s while en route to the target. In a series of engagements, the yellow-nosed Mustangs claimed 11 jets damaged, but no victories. Sloan's kill on the 9th also proved to be the 361st's last aerial success in World War 2.

The final Me 262 victory on 9 April was claimed by the CO of the 343rd FS/55th FG, Maj Edward B Giller, who was leading his unit as part of the group-strength escort for bombers from the 3rd Air Division that were targeting the airfield at Oberweisenfeld, near Munich. Whilst patrolling near Ingolstadt, four Me 262s attacked the bomber stream and then fled the area. Shortly thereafter, Giller spotted a lone jet fighter descending through 20,000 ft with two P-51s vainly attempting to overhaul it. Using his height advantage, Giller joined the pursuit;

'I followed him for ten minutes, with the 262 doing a very gentle turn to the left and losing altitude. We were now over the southern edge of Munich, with the German jet at 1000 ft and me still at 7000 ft. Going balls out, I caught him at 50 ft just over the perimeter track [at Munich-Riem airfield]. He was going west to east about 100 yards to the right of the runway. I fired several bursts and observed strikes on the left wing root and fuselage. Looking back, I watched him crash-land on the field 100 yards to the right of the runway in a large cloud of dust and flying pieces. He didn't burn, which I assume was due to the fact he was out of fuel.'

Minutes later, Giller found a large number of aircraft hidden in the woods on either side of the main autobahn south of Munich. In the ensuing melee more than 50 enemy aeroplanes were claimed to have been destroyed by the 55th FG, with Giller being credited with three strafing victories – including an Me 262. By VE Day his tally stood at three aerial (two in the P-38) and six strafing kills.

On the afternoon of 10 April the Allies launched 1232 bombers covered by more than 900 fighters. The targets were airfields, transportation hubs and military infrastructure centres in Oranienburg, Rechlin, Neuruppin, Stendal, Brandenburg-Briest, Zerbst, Burg, Parchim and Wittenberge. A number of German fighters were scrambled in response to this armada, with JG 7 sending 55 Me 262s aloft – many of which were armed with 24 R4M rockets apiece – from all three *Gruppen*.

One flight of seven Me 262s, led by high-scoring ace Oberleutnant Walter Schuck of 3./JG 7, was patrolling at 24,000 ft when they were directed towards Oranienburg, where a formation of B-17s was approaching from the northwest. As they made their way towards Oranienburg, the jets climbed to 30,000 ft. At 1430 hrs Schuck and his flight bounced the Flying Fortresses just as they dropped their bombs on Oranienburg, the German ace closing to within 300 yards of his first victim before opening fire with his four 30 mm cannon. One of the B-17's wings disintegrated under the weight of the fire. Schuck then pulled up and went after another bomber, hitting it hard and sending it down in a spin. Several crew members bailed out. In rapid succession Schuck shot down two more B-17s, taking his tally to 206 victories. The veteran ace had taken just eight minutes to destroy four Flying Fortresses. Moments later Schuck was himself shot down, almost certainly by Capt Joseph A Peterburs of the 55th FS/20th FG, who subsequently fell victim to flak while strafing an airfield minutes after he had despatched Schuck's jet. Both pilots survived the war and would meet decades later.

A total of six Me 262s were claimed as destroyed by the 20th FG, which emerged as the highest scoring group in terms of jet kills on 10 April. Both the 352nd and 353rd FGs claimed three apiece, with two of the pilots from the latter group achieving ace status with their respective Me 262 victories. The first to claim his fifth kill was Capt Gordon B Compton from the 351st FS, who, that day, was leading 'Lawyer Red' Flight on an escort mission to Zerbst airfield in northern Germany when he heard a report of jet activity over Dessau five miles to the south. Turning his flight in that direction, Compton flew several orbits over the city from 1400 hrs until he spotted an Me 262 on the deck heading east;

'I started a dive from about 10,000 ft and pulled up along the left side of the Me 262, which was turning left now, to make sure it wasn't a P-51. I then tacked onto its tail and shot it up a bit. The jet caught fire and crashed on the edge of Köthen airdrome.'

Compton's wingman, 2Lt James L McDermott, confirmed the victory and actually saw the jet hit a telephone pole before it crashed. This kill took Compton's final tally of aerial victories to 5.5, and doubled his haul of Me 262s – he had claimed his first on 22 February. He was also credited with 15 strafing kills, and had scored his early victories in the P-47.

The second pilot to 'make ace' that day was Capt Robert W Abernathy of the 350th FS, who had claimed a single kill with the Thunderbolt before his squadron switched to P-51s. The Me 262 was his fifth, and last, victory. Non-aces from the 4th, 55th, 56th, 356th, 359th and 364th FGs were also credited with Me 262 kills on 10 April, with no fewer than 27 fighter pilots from nine Eighth Air Force fighter groups downing 21 Messerschmitt jets in aerial combat. This tally made it the deadliest day of aerial combat for the Me 262. However, this score had come at a price, for the Me 262 force – which launched 76 sorties – had claimed 27 aerial victories, including eight P-51s.

No further Me 262s were shot down until 14 April, when a pair of jets were claimed by two aces from the Ninth Air Force's 354th FG.

Capt Clayton K Gross had scored his first aerial victory on 11 May 1944 and 'made ace' on 29 October. On 14 April he was leading a flight of Mustangs from the 355th FS in his assigned aircraft, P-51D 44-63668 *LIVE BAIT*, when he spotted a lone Me 262A-1b near Alt Lönnewitz airfield and split-essed into a full throttle dive from 12,000 ft in pursuit of the aeroplane.

As the Mustang passed through 450 mph it was suddenly gripped by compressibility. For several harrowing seconds Gross struggled to pull the fighter out of the dive. When he finally levelled out the Me 262 was right in front of him, but his overtake speed was so high that he only managed a quick, albeit well-aimed, burst that blew off the jet's left wingtip. Gross pulled up into a chandelle to the right, and as he came around he saw the jet going straight up with its left engine on fire. Using what little energy he had left from the dive, he followed the jet into the climb and watched the pilot bail out as the Me 262 slowed and fell into a tail slide. As Gross watched the pilot's parachute open, every flak battery on the airfield opened up on him. Quickly gathering his flight together, he fled the area.

There is conflicting evidence as to who was flying the Me 262 claimed by Gross, although it seems almost certain that 19-year-old Gefreiter Kurt Lobgesang of 1./JG 7 was at the controls. The two would meet 50 years later. This was Capt Gross's sixth, and final, victory of the war.

The second jet was shot down by 1Lt Loyd J Overfield, a nine-victory ace with the 353rd FS. It had taken the 26-year-old just three missions to claim five aerial kills, with three of his victories coming on 7 August 1944 when he downed a trio of Bf 109s over Mayenne, in northwestern France. On 14 April, Overfield was flying along the Elbe River north of Dresden when he spotted three Me 262s heading south, but was unable give chase. However, he did come upon a He 111, which he quickly sent down in flames. Overfield then spotted another Me 262 six miles south of the city, and after a brief chase he fired several bursts that set the jet on fire, forcing the pilot to bail out. This pair of victories brought Overfield's final tally to 11.

As the war drew to its inevitable conclusion, the Me 262s valiantly continued to counter Allied bombing raids. On 17 April Capt Richard Hewitt and his wingman, multiple jet-killer 1Lt Allen Rosenblum, from Duxford's 82nd FS/78th FG chased a pair of Me 262s to Kralupy airfield near Prague, where Hewitt shot one of the jets down when it was on short finals to land. Rosenblum was in turn forced to crash-land minutes later after his fighter was hit in the engine by flak whilst strafing. With his wingman a PoW and his own gun camera film inconclusive, Hewitt failed to have his all-important fifth victory claim confirmed. He was at the controls of his distinctively marked P-51D-20 (44-64147) when he downed his Me 262 (*USAAF*)

Capt Charles E Weaver (seen here to the right) of the 362nd FS/357th FG downed an Me 262 over Prague-Ruzyne airfield on 18 April whilst flying this machine, P-51D-20 44-72199. Although the Mustang lacked a name, it did feature what was possibly the most striking nose art applied to any 357th FG aircraft during World War 2 – nudes were rarely seen on USAAF fighters in the European Theatre of Operations. The Me 262 was Weaver's eighth, and last, aerial victory, the ace completing 73 missions between August 1944 and May 1945. 44-72199, minus its reclining female, was sold to the Swiss Air Force post-war (*Lt Col Clarence 'Bud' Anderson*)

On 16 April 1Lts Vernon O Fein and Henry A Yandel each claimed an Me 262 destroyed to give the P-47-equipped 368th FG, assigned to the Ninth Air Force, its only jet victories of the conflict – both pilots were from the 397th FS. A third Me 262 was credited to Maj Eugene E Ryan, who had been made CO of the 55th FG's 338th FS just three days earlier. He had claimed the victory (his third, and last, aerial success) during an escort mission to Salzburg, in Austria, downing the fighter over nearby Hörsching airfield. Ryan was also credited with an He 111 destroyed in a strafing attack on this mission.

Six Me 262s were claimed as shot down by USAAF fighters on 17 April, with five falling to Mustang pilots from the 339th, 354th, 357th and 364th FGs and one to 1Lt James Zweizig flying a P-47 from the 404th FS/371st FG. None of these aviators were aerial aces, although the victory for Capt Roy W Orndorff of the 364th FG's 383rd FS (one of two Me 262s credited to the squadron that day) took his tally to four – he also had four strafing kills.

A seventh success went unconfirmed from the 17th involving Capt Richard Hewitt and his wingman, multiple jet killer 1Lt Allen Rosenblum, of the 82nd FS/78th FG. They had chased a pair of Me 262s towards Kralupy airfield, near Prague, in Czechoslovakia. One of the jets was on short finals to land when Hewitt's 0.50-cal rounds hit home and sent it down in flames just short of the runway. The engine in Rosenblum's P-51 was then hit by flak and started to burn, but he was not quite finished inflicting damage on the Luftwaffe. Rosenblum strafed an unidentified trainer and then somehow survived a 300 mph belly landing that saw his Mustang smash through two hedgerows and a stand of trees.

With no clear gun camera film and a wingman who was now a PoW, Hewitt's victory could not be, and has never been, confirmed, thus officially depriving him of ace status – he had claimed aerial victories on 16 March and 21 November 1944 and two on 19 March 1945, plus 4.333 strafing kills.

The following day (18 April) three more Me 262s were credited to USAAF fighter pilots, two of whom were aces from the 357th FG.

Double ace and jet killer Maj Donald H Bochkay scored his second Me 262 victory when he bounced one over Prague on 18 April. Although he hit the fighter's right engine, the German pilot was still able to break right into a very tight 9G turn, which Bochkay somehow managed to match in his P-51D-20 44-72244 (not the aeroplane seen here, which is his P-51B-5 43-6963). Closing to 250 yards at 475 mph, Bochkay fired again and set the jet on fire. His Encounter Report duly noted, 'His tail came off. It then rolled over and went in like a torch'. The Me 262 took Maj Bochkay's final tally to 13.833 aerial victories (*Peter Randall collection*)

Acknowledging the continuing threat posed by the Me 262s to its heavy bombers, the Eighth Air Force had briefed the 357th FG to cover the airfields near Prague an hour before the arrival of B-17s and B-24s. Since the Me 262 had limited endurance, the plan was to either knock them out as they took off or strafe them on the ground. High-scoring ace Maj Kit Carson of the 362nd FS led the mission. Through some superb navigation the group was able to fly a zigzag course at low altitude to disguise its intentions. It hit Prague-Ruzyne airfield at exactly 1300 hrs, at which point Carson despatched Maj Don Bochkay to cover the two nearby fields, then orbited Prague-Ruzyne to see what the German fighter pilots would do. Soon, the Mustang pilots saw the jets taxi out for takeoff. Carson later wrote;

'As the first '262 started his take-off roll we dropped our wing tanks and I started down with "Red" Flight from 13,000 ft with an easy wing-over. The '262 pilot had his gear up and was going past the field boundary when we ploughed through intense light flak. As I came astern of him and levelled off at 400+ mph, I firewalled it to hold my speed and centred the bull's eye of the optical sight on the fuselage and hit him with a two-second burst.'

Carson's timing was slightly off, for although he scored strikes he only claimed the jet as damaged. Capt Chuck Weaver of the 362nd FS had better luck, catching an Me 262 trying to land. He shot it down for his eighth, and last, aerial victory, the wreckage landing on the field. He and 1Lt Oscar Ridley had both gone after the Me 262 as it drew the Mustangs across the airfield. This resulted in them being targeted by 'considerable flak', related Weaver. 'Lt Ridley called that he had been hit. I returned to the field and told him to fly west for as long as possible. I caught up with him at a point 20 miles west of Prague. His engine was smoking badly. He said the fire was bad and he was leaving the aeroplane. He bailed out at 5000 ft. His 'chute opened successfully'. Ridley was the last pilot to be lost by the group as a result of enemy action.

Bochkay, meanwhile, was leading the 363rd's 'Cement Blue' Flight when he heard 'White' Flight call in a bogey at '11 o'clock low'. The ace recalled;

'I recognised it as an Me 262. I dropped my tanks and dove from 15,000 ft to 13,000 ft, pulling up behind the jet. I then let him have a burst from 400 yards, getting very good hits on his right jet unit and canopy. He then broke right in a very tight diving turn, pulling streamers from his wingtips. My "G"-meter read 9Gs. As he straightened out at 7000 ft, I was 250 yards behind him, going at 475 mph. I let him have another burst, getting very good hits on his right jet unit again. He then popped his canopy as I let him have another burst. Large pieces came off his ship and it caught fire. I pulled off to miss the pieces and watched the Me 262 fall apart. His tail came off. It then rolled over and went in like a torch, crashing into some woods next to a river. The pilot never got out.'

Capt Ernest C Tiede Jnr and 2Lt Gifford W Miller both confirmed Bochkay's final victory, which took his tally to 13.833.

The third victory on 18 April was claimed by Maj Ralph F Johnson, CO of the 325 FG's 319th FS. This Mustang unit was assigned to the Fifteenth Air Force, and his victory was the last of 11 Me 262s credited to fighter groups flying from Italy.

A fourth jet victory was claimed on 18 April when Lt Col Dale Shafer, CO of the 339th FG's 503rd FS, downed an Ar 234 near Regensburg. He was the only pilot of the 14 from the group credited with jet kills during World War 2 to 'make ace'. Four of Shafer's seven aerial victories came whilst he was flying Spitfire Vs and IXs with the 309th FS/31st FG in North Africa and the Mediterranean in 1942-44.

Over the next week, the last 11 Me 262s credited to USAAF fighters in aerial combat fell to non-aces – six of them on 19 April to pilots from the 357th FG. These were the final jet victories claimed by the group, and it raised the unit's overall score to 19 Me 262s destroyed. The 357th was undoubtedly the USAAF's most effective jet-killing group.

On 25 April the 479th FG became the second of only two USAAF fighter groups to claim victories over all three Luftwaffe jet types. That morning the 434th FS was participating in a bomber escort mission to Traunstein, in Bavaria. Flying at 24,000 ft, 'Newcross Blue' Flight had just commenced a 360-degree turn over the target when, part way through the manoeuvre, 'Newcross Blue Three' – 1Lt Hilton O Thompson (whose only other victory had been an Me 262 downed on 7 April), spotted a

Although 14 pilots from the 339th FG combined to shoot down 12 Me 262s and an Ar 234, only one of them 'made ace' – Lt Col Dale E Shafer. No details have been found about the action, which took place at 1225 hrs on 18 April near Regensburg. Shafer, CO of the 503rd FS, was at the controls of his assigned P-51D-20 44-72147 at the time (he had downed an Fw 190D-9 and damaged a second in it on 18 March), the Ar 234 being his seventh, and final, victory of the war (*Peter Randall collection*)

In the final weeks of the war in Europe Twelfth Air Force B-26s fought a series of vicious battles with the Me 262s from Generalleutnant Adolf Galland's JV 44. On 26 April, Galland and his wingman attacked 17th BG Marauders over Ulm and shot down one bomber. As the high-scoring ace flew by the 34th BS B-26 flown by Maj Luther W Gurkin, his waist gunner, TSgt Henry Dietz, fired a quick burst that heavily damaged the fuel tanks in Galland's fighter. Dietz is seen here standing third from the right (*Robert Forsyth collection*)

bogey 2000 ft above them heading east. Thompson immediately set off in pursuit of the bogey with his wingman and a spare aircraft. Thompson's Encounter Report describes what subsequently happened;

'The jet turned to a southeasterly direction and I closed to 800 yards at his level. Ranging with my K-14 sight, I fired two short bursts and observed hits around his left engine. Then I began closing rapidly from "seven o'clock astern" and fired several bursts from 600 yards down to 300 yards, observing strikes along the entire left side of the fuselage, which caused many pieces to fall off. At 200 yards I pulled to the right and watched him spiral down at a 40-degree angle.'

The Ar 234 pilot bailed out of his stricken bomber, which crashed in the vicinity of Berchtesgaden. Thompson's Arado was the 15th, and final, Ar 234 shot down by the USAAF, and the last jet victory for the 479th. The group was credited with downing an Me 163, three Me 262s and an Ar 234.

Just before 1700 hrs that same day (25 April), a formation of 13 JV 44 jets, including Me 262A-1a/U4 Wk-Nr 111899, which was armed with a single 50 mm Mauser MK 214 cannon, took off from Munich-Riem. The aircraft split into two formations, with one heading out on a freelance patrol against the hundreds of American fighters roaming over southern Germany and the other flying south to attack B-26s of the 344th BG that were targeting Erding airfield and a nearby ordnance depot. However, all five jets looking for enemy fighters aborted for various reasons. Three of the remaining aircraft, including the Me 262A-1a/U4 flown by 72-victory nightfighter ace Major Willi Herget, succeeded in attacking the Marauders prior to being intercepted by P-51s from the Ninth Air Force's 370th FG. A single Me 262 was downed by the group, 1Lts Richard D Stevenson and Robert W Hoyle of the 402nd FS sharing in its destruction. Their victory was the 17th Me 262 to fall to Ninth Air Force fighters, Capt Jerry G Mast and 2Lt William H Myers of the 365th FG's 388th FS having shared the 16th 24 hours earlier in their P-47s.

On 26 April, the B-26-equipped 42nd BW launched a maximum effort against Lechfeld airfield with fragmentation bombs. As the wing headed into Bavaria JV 44 was put on alert, and at 1120 hrs Generalleutnant Adolf Galland led a scramble of five Me 262s from Munich-Riem. Once airborne, they were vectored towards Ulm, where they would clash with the Thunderbolts of the 27th and 50th FGs. Galland and his *Experten* approached the bombers head-on at 11,000 ft, passed over them and then made a wide sweeping turn, before returning to attack the Marauders from 'eight o'clock'. Galland's wingman, Unteroffizier Eduard Schallmoser, flying Me 262 'White 14', launched his R4M rockets and was transfixed when a Marauder 'blew apart in the air'. On the same pass, Galland armed his quartet of 30 mm Mk 108s and switched off the safety for his R4Ms. He opened fire with his cannon, disintegrating another bomber and heavily damaging a second. He then attempted to fire his rockets, but he had forgotten to turn off the second safety switch!

While Galland and Schallmoser were boring in on the Marauders, SSgt Donald P Edelen, flight engineer/top turret gunner aboard Maj Luther Gurkin's B-26, which was leading the 17th BG's 34th BS, saw a flash out of the corner of his eye and called waist gunner TSgt Henry Dietz to check 'nine o'clock level' to see if he saw anything. Dietz replied in the negative, but then Edelen's world went into surreal slow motion. Seconds after Dietz had said he could not see anything, Edelen heard a quick burst from a 0.50-cal, followed by Dietz exclaiming 'I got one!' over the intercom. Then, from his turret, Edelen looked Eduard Schallmoser right in the eye as he sped past the Marauder. After realising his rockets were not armed, Galland fired a quick burst at a third Marauder and broke left just as the rounds from TSgt Dietz's machine gun struck the fuel tanks of the Generalleutnant's Me 262.

The P-47-equipped 50th FG had been tasked with escorting B-26s of the French 11e *Brigade de Bombardment,* and among the pilots aloft that day was 1Lt James J Finnegan of the 10th FS. Leading 'Green' Flight in his assigned P-47D 42-28453 *The Irish Shillalah*, he had not seen any jets up to this point in his tour. This all changed when someone called 'Jet bandits!' over the radio and Finnegan looked around just in time to see two B-26s explode and two 'darts' streak through the bomber formation and break left and right. He decided to go after the jet on the left;

'I turned over on my back, pulled tight on the stick and almost immediately had the enemy aircraft in my sights. I got off two quick bursts but couldn't see if I had hit anything because the nose of my aircraft was pulled too high to get a good lead. However, I dropped my nose and observed what I thought were bits and pieces coming from the cowling. In addition, I saw smoke trailing from the wing.'

After the war Galland recalled the damage Finnegan's burst had done to his already ailing Me 262;

Just as JV 44 struck the B-26s from the 34th BS, 1Lt James J Finnegan of the 10th FS/50th FG heard the warning 'Jet bandits!' over the radio. He looked down in time to see two Marauders explode and an Me 262 diving away streaming fuel. Finnegan dived on Galland's jet and fired two bursts that blew off the Me 262's engine cowlings, shattered its instrument panel and wounded the pilot in the right knee (*Robert Forsyth collection*)

During the 25 April engagement with Generalleutnant Galland, 1Lt Finnegan was flying P-47D-28 42-28453 *The Irish Shillalah*. The downing of the Me 262 gave Finnegan his second kill. Although Galland's Me 262 was destroyed when it crash-landed at Munich-Riem, neither TSgt Dietz nor 1Lt Finnegan were officially credited with a confirmed victory (*Robert Forsyth collection*)

'A hail of fire enveloped me. A sharp rap hit my right knee, the instrument panel with its indispensable instruments was shattered, the right engine was also hit – its metal covering worked loose in the wind and was partly carried away – and now the left engine was hit. I could hardly hold her in the air.'

In an amazing feat of airmanship Galland made it back to his airfield, and despite it being strafed by P-47s as he approached, the veteran fighter ace was able to belly-land his Me 262 on to the grass and run for cover. Although Finnegan claimed a probable and 'thought no more of it', history has credited him and TSgt Dietz with shooting down the famed 'General of Fighter Pilots'.

Although Galland was out of the fight, the battle between JV 44 and the 50th FG raged on. While Finnegan was pursuing Galland, Capt Robert W Clark shot down another jet, with the pilot bailing out. In the brief and intense action, JV 44 had destroyed three B-26s – two from the 34th BS and one from the 95th BS. There were no survivors. Aside from a probable claim back on 26 November 1944 and Finnegan's unofficial shared victory over Galland, Clark's Me 262 was the only confirmed jet victory for the 50th FG.

Just before noon on 26 April Thunderbolts from the 27th FG were on a fighter sweep over Munich when Capt Herbert A Philo and his wingman spotted a lone Me 262 right in front of them just as they were about to strafe a ground target. The jet was right down on the deck when Philo came in and fired a burst that immediately sent the Me 262 crashing in flames. This was the only victory for Capt Philo, the sole jet victory for the 27th FG and the USAAF's last confirmed jet victory of the war. However, there were still a few skirmishes, some of them deadly, to be fought in the final week of the war.

After Galland was shot down, command of JV 44 was passed to Oberstleutnant Heinz Bär, whose 200+ victory tally included 15 kills in the Me 262. On 27 April he was flying the six-cannon Me 262A-1/U5 when he led Unteroffizier Franz Köster and Major Willi Herget on a patrol that saw them get into a scrap with several flights of P-47s. Bär and Köster each claimed two Thunderbolts destroyed apiece – these victories gave Köster ace status, with six kills – and Herget recorded his 73rd, and last, success. Two days later Bär shot down another Thunderbolt while flying the Me 262A-1/U5 on what was almost certainly JV 44's last operational sortie.

On 1 May Ninth Air Force P-47 pilots Capt James H Hall and 1Lt Joseph Richlitsky from the 367th FS/358th FG claimed an Me 262 as shared damaged. Two days later, the final jet encounter took place when 1Lts Arnold G Sarrow and Albert T Kalvaitis of the 365th FG damaged an Me 262 over Prague.

CHAPTER SIX

ALL THE KING'S MEN

When the Luftwaffe first deployed its new Me 262 jet bombers to France during the latter stage of the Normandy campaign, it was in very small numbers. They were quickly swept up in the retreat and there were no encounters with Allied fighters. However, as the invasion force pushed north into Belgium in late August 1944 there were occasional sightings, and the first German jet to be shot down fell to P-47Ds of the 78th FG on the 28th as described in Chapter Two. It was during the desperate fighting over the bridges in Holland, which had been audaciously seized in the ill-fated Operation *Market Garden* in late September, that jets ominously began to be seen.

During the early evening of 26 September, veteran ace Wg Cdr Geoffrey Page, Wing Leader of No 125 Wing, led another patrol to the Nijmegen area. During the course of the mission Flg Off Frank Campbell (who had four victories to his name) of No 132 Sqn, flying Spitfire IX PL257/FF-T, spotted an Me 262 that he chased and managed to damage before it flew off at high speed. Campbell's close encounter gave the 2nd Tactical Air Force (TAF) its first claim against the Me 262. Two days later, Flt Lt James 'Chips' McColl (who was credited with three victories) of Spitfire IX-equipped No 416 Sqn damaged another near Nijmegen, whilst on the 30th No 441 Sqn ace Flg Off Ron Lake, again in a Spitfire IX, also damaged an Me 262.

On 1 October the Tempest Vs of No 122 Wing, led by Wg Cdr John Wray, arrived at B80 Volkel, the most forward Allied airfield in newly-

All three of Wg Cdr John Wray's jet claims came whilst he was flying his personal Tempest V EJ750/JBW. This aeroplane was subsequently written off in February 1945 when its pilot was forced to crash-land after being hit by flak. The fighter had by then been passed on to No 486 Sqn (*Chris Thomas collection*)

Whilst leading Spitfires of No 401 Sqn on 5 October 1944, Sqn Ldr Rod Smith helped shoot down the first Me 262 to fall to a Commonwealth unit. His quarter-share in the jet's demise proved to be the Malta ace's final claim (*DND*)

liberated Holland. Later that same day pilots from the wing had their first sightings of their new jet-powered foe, and a system of patrols was swiftly established. These proved inconclusive, however, as the Me 262s were easily able to draw away from the Tempest Vs.

During a sweep over Holland four days later, 12 Spitfire IXs (all fitted with the latest gyro gunsight) from No 401 Sqn, led by gunnery expert and 13-victory ace Sqn Ldr Rod Smith, were near Nijmegen when, at 1430 hrs, they spotted a Me 262 from 5./KG(J) 51 flown by Hauptmann Hans-Christoph Buttmann. Several of the Spitfires attacked, as Smith wrote later;

'I sighted an Me 262 coming head on 500 ft below. He went into a port climbing turn and I turned to starboard after him, along with several other Spitfires. He then dived down towards the bridge, twisting and turning and half-rolling at very high speed. He then flew across Nijmegen, turning from side to side. I saw a Spitfire get some strikes on him and he streamed white smoke from the starboard wing root. He flew on at very high speed still, and I managed to get behind him and fire two three-second bursts from approximately 200-300 yards. He zoomed very high and I saw strikes on him in the port and starboard nacelles. A small fire started in the starboard nacelle and a big one in the port nacelle while I was firing. I broke down to starboard under him and he turned down to starboard behind me. I thought at the time he was trying to attack me, even though in flames. He passed behind me and crashed in a field southwest of Nijmegen.'

Other pilots from Smith's section had also attacked Buttmann's jet, including Flg Off John MacKay, a future 13-victory ace, Flg Off Gus Sinclair, who claimed the Me 262 as his fourth, and last, success, Flt Lt Hedley 'Snooks' Everard, who was already an ace, and Flt Lt Robert 'Tex' Davenport, for whom the 'share' took him to acedom. More significantly, Buttmann's Me 262 was the first jet to be shot down by a Commonwealth squadron.

Tempest V pilots were also increasingly seeing Me 262s along the German border with Holland, and on 13 October V1 ace Plt Off Bob Cole of No 3 Sqn claimed the first jet victory for the Hawker fighter. Whilst flying north of Aachen in JN868, he spotted the Me 262 flown by Unteroffizier Edmund Delatowski of 3./KG 51 and dived on the unsuspecting jet. Despite coaxing his fighter up to 480 mph, Cole was unable to close the distance. However, Delatowski's jet then inexplicably slowed, and the RAF pilot took his chance;

'I closed in to about 500 yards and fired one short burst, dead astern, which missed. I closed in to about 150 yards, still dead astern, and fired another short burst. The enemy aircraft immediately exploded just as a doodlebug does and many pieces flew off, including what looked like a plank six feet long.'

The injured Edmund Delatowski somehow managed to bail out.

That same day Flt Lt Tony Seager (who would be credited with two victories) damaged an Me 262 over Grave, in Holland, for No 80 Sqn's first

claim against a jet. These were, however, isolated successes, although 2nd TAF fighters often forced the jets to jettison their bombs and turn back. In order to increase its pilots' chances of success, No 122 Wing decided to have a small number of manned Tempest Vs on standby at Volkel, ready to scramble for the jets' bases so as to catch them at their most vulnerable when approaching to land short of fuel at mission-end. In response, the Luftwaffe positioned 'flak lanes' around its airfields and mounted its own defensive patrols with Fw 190s and Bf 109s.

During one such airfield patrol on 3 November, the No 122 Wing Leader Wg Cdr Wray, in his personal Tempest EJ750/JBW, spotted two Me 262s flying southwest whilst he was at 18,000 ft. On sighting him, the enemy pilots turned back. Wray, using his height advantage, dived after the right-hand jet, and, closing at high speed, opened fire 'before he got out of range. Suddenly a large piece flew off the aircraft and he flicked over on to his back and disappeared downwards into cloud in an inverted position. I followed, but the thickness of the cloud made it impossible for me to maintain contact'. Although John Wray claimed the Me 262 as damaged, Oberfähnrich Willi Banzhoff of *Kommando* 'Nowotny' crashed near Hittfeld and was killed. That same day other patrols strafed and damaged jets on their airfields near Osnabrück, such as Rheine and Bramsche.

By now the Luftwaffe was increasingly using the Me 262 as a defensive fighter, rather than as a bomber, resulting in some of the daylight raids by Bomber Command Lancasters and Halifaxes being intercepted by them – such as on 27 November when Spitfire IXs of No 1 Sqn escorting a Lancaster raid on Dortmund spotted jets for the first time. Tempest V pilots also engaged more jets in early December, the first of these encounters occurring on the 3rd when Flt Lt John 'Judy' Garland of No 80 Sqn spotted an aircraft flying at low level whilst he was attacking a train near Rheine;

'I identified it as an Me 262. I closed to 400 yards and the Hun turned sharply to port, climbing to approximately 150 ft. The jet then appeared

RAF intelligence staff sift through the shattered wreckage of Hauptmann Hans-Christoph Buttmann's Me 262 five miles northeast of Nijmegen. The personnel on the right have rigged up a pump in an attempt to drain the water-filled crater created by the 5./KG(J) 51 machine when it crashed (*© IWM CL 1350*)

The Wing Leader of Tempest-equipped No 122 Wg was Wg Cdr John Wray, whose only air combat successes were both against German jets. Although he was awarded a damaged claim following his first encounter with a Messerschmitt jet on 3 November 1944, he had in fact shot the Me 262 down. Wray was credited with destroying his second Me 262, on 17 December, however. Finally, Wray damaged an Ar 234 on Christmas Day, this aeroplane also being wrecked in the subsequent crash-landing (*Chris Thomas collection*)

to do a high-speed stall, followed by a complete flick roll. As he straightened up, the cockpit hood flew off. Closing to 150 yards, I fired one one-second burst but saw no strikes. The enemy aircraft immediately went into a flat spin to port and crashed into a small wood.'

The Me 262 was from I./KG(J) 51, and its pilot, Knight's Cross holder Oberleutnant Hans-Joachim Valet, was killed. Garland would subsequently claim an additional three victories before VE Day.

Flying from B88 Heesch five days later (8 December), No 442 Sqn pilots on an armed reconnaissance mission over enemy territory optimistically chased a trio of Me 262s in their Spitfire IXs but were unable to catch them. However, on the 10th, No 56 Sqn's Flt Sgt Jackson attacked Leutnant Walter Roth's Me 262 Wk-Nr 170281 of I./KG(J) 51 in his Tempest V, claiming the aeroplane as damaged when, in fact, the jet crash-landed.

One week later, Wg Cdr John Wray attacked his second Me 262 when, on the morning of the 17th, he was warned of jets in the area and sighted two aeroplanes from 11./KG(J) 51 near the River Rhine. Ordering his wingman after the No 2, he pursued Me 262A-2a Wk-Nr 110501/9K+BP flown by Leutnant Wolfgang Lübke, who was at low level. The No 122 Wing Leader subsequently wrote;

'I was going flat out at about 450 mph, but losing ground. He was about 200 yards ahead, but drawing away. The visibility was not too good at the time, and I realised that I might lose him. I opened fire, and fired about a four-second burst, but with no apparent results. I had hoped to at least get him weaving. Then he started to turn slowly, so I set off again. By this time he was right on the deck, and I was slightly above him, and found that I was catching him up. I opened fire again, and there appeared to be strikes on the wings. He started to weave violently, which was not too clever at that altitude, but this allowed me to close to about 300 yards. I was about to fire again when his port wingtip hit a building on the edge of the Rhine and he pitched straight into the river.'

This was Wray's second success against a jet in six weeks, his victory coinciding with the German offensive in the Ardennes that saw a spike in enemy air activity and increasing encounters with jets whenever the dreadful winter weather allowed. An improvement in conditions saw aerial action continue over the Christmas period, which resulted in some rewarding 'presents' for several units.

At midday on Christmas Day, Spitfire IXs of No 411 Sqn were flying in support of US ground forces around Bastogne, in Belgium, when the engine in the aircraft of Flt Lt Jack Boyle's wingman began misfiring. Both pilots duly broke off from the rest of the unit and headed back to Heesch. As they approached the airfield Boyle spotted an Me 262 beneath him. He dived and, with his speed registering in excess of 500 mph, opened fire and hit one of the jet's engines;

'He immediately dived for the deck as an evasive tactic, but with only one engine he couldn't outrun me. I scored several more hits before he clipped some tall tree tops and then hit the ground at an almost flat angle. His aircraft disintegrated in stages from nose to tail as it ripped up the turf for several hundred yards until only the tailplane assembly was left, and it went cartwheeling along just below me and at about my speed. Fire and smoke marked his trail.'

Oberleutnant Hans-Georg Lamle of I./KG(J) 51, who had just bombed Allied forces in the Belgian city of Liège, was killed. His demise gave Boyle the second of his six victories.

Several hours later, Spitfire XVIs from No 403 Sqn, led by Sqn Ldr Jim Collier, were out for a patrol over Malmedy, in Belgium, when they came across a *Kette* of three Me 262s flying in large circles southwest of Aachen, on the German border. As the Spitfires approached, two of them made off under full power, but the third continued circling, apparently unaware of the impending threat. As Collier came within range he opened fire, observing strikes on one wing. The enemy pilot then attempted to escape, but Collier maintained his position and continued to fire, seeing white smoke beginning to stream from the Me 262's left engine. The jet then slowly rolled on to its back and its pilot, Feldwebel Hans Meyer of I./KG(J) 51, bailed out before his aeroplane crashed. Collier's notable victory was his fifth claim, of which three were aircraft destroyed.

At the same time as Collier was scoring his final kill, eight Tempest Vs of No 486 Sqn were patrolling nearby, and Flt Lt Jack Stafford, a V1 ace, made his first step to acedom against manned aircraft when he too spotted an Me 262;

'I broke up towards him and commenced firing at extreme range. I maintained my fire up to about 400 yards, and I saw pieces fall away from his port unit. As the enemy aircraft passed overhead, several red balls fell from it and he was slowed considerably. I fired and it commenced diving, leaving a trail of white smoke. He then rolled on his back and I saw the pilot bail out, observing that his parachute did not open properly.'

Stafford's No 2 was fellow V1 ace Plt Off Duff Bremner, who also attacked the jet;

'I got into line astern and fired a two-second burst from 600 yards, and this time saw streams of white vapour coming from his port unit. I fired another burst from line astern – this time at 800 yards. The Me 262 increased his angle of dive, rolled onto its back and the pilot bailed out.'

Both Tempest V pilots were credited with a shared victory each, although the similarity of their reports with that of Sqn Ldr Collier's leaves the possibility that all three had attacked the unfortunate Meyer, with both the Canadians and New Zealanders being unaware of each other's presence. Either way, both units were able to celebrate a successful Christmas.

German jets were also encountered on Boxing Day as the dangerous German Ardennes offensive ground to a halt in the snow. The CO of Spitfire XVI-equipped No 127 Sqn, ace Sqn Ldr Ralph 'Sammy' Sampson, spotted some near Enschede, in Holland, but his frustration at being unable to catch them was evident in his mission report;

'There were some jet jobs reported and then we saw four Me 262s, but we had no hope of catching them. I had a long range squirt from 1500 yards, but more in desperation than with any sense of hitting one.'

Future six-victory ace Flt Lt Johnny Boyle of No 411 Sqn shot down the Me 262 of I./KG(J) 51's Oberleutnant Hans-Georg Lamle on Christmas Day after shepherding his wingman back to B88 Heesch (*PAC*)

Flt Lt Johnny Boyle was flying Spitfire IX MK686/DB-L of No 411 Sqn on Christmas Day 1944 when he shot down Oberleutnant Lamle's Me 262 (*PAC*)

However, near the border town of Julich, Flt Lt Elgin 'Irish' Ireland of Spitfire IX-equipped No 411 Sqn managed to damage an Me 262 (his remaining three claims were for victories), as, in mid-afternoon, did the No 135 Wing Leader Wg Cdr Ray Harries in his Spitfire IX – the 'damaged' was the last claim for the 16-victory ace.

'The New Year started with a bang.' Thus, with something of an understatement, did No 401 Sqn's diarist begin the entry for 1945 as its base at Heesch came under aerial attack at dawn. Operation *Bodenplatte* was a massive, but ultimately costly, Luftwaffe attack on Allied airfields that resulted in a day of heavy fighting. The valuable jets were not involved, however, and having achieved acedom earlier in the day, recently promoted Flt Lt John MacKay of No 401 Sqn led a section in an anti-jet 'Rat Hunt' to Rheine airfield at 1535 hrs. Several more piston-engined fighters were duly claimed, and MacKay and his wingman, Flt Sgt A K Woodill, also damaged a jet. The latter was spared, however, when MacKay's cannon jammed and his wingman ran out of ammunition.

It was not only tactical fighters that encountered the Luftwaffe jets, whose performance meant they were ideal for chasing high-flying Mosquito and Spitfire reconnaissance aircraft. During the early afternoon of 14 January, a Spitfire PR XI of No 16 Sqn being flown by Flg Off W F 'Barry' Barker on a reconnaissance mission of the Dusseldorf area was intercepted by an Me 163 Komet. Barker evaded so violently that he believed the fighter crashed.

That same day the Jadgwaffe suffered a crippling defeat, losing almost 200 aircraft to USAAF and RAF escort fighters during daylight bombing raids. 2nd TAF fighter sweeps also took a toll. During a sweep by the

Tempest V EJ523/SA-D was the mount of New Zealand V1 ace Plt Off Duff Bremner of No 486 Sqn when he shared in the destruction of an Me 262 near Aachen on Christmas Day 1944. EJ523 did not survive the war, being wrecked in a crash landing on 25 February 1945 (*Chris Thomas collection*)

Norwegians of Spitfire IX-equipped No 132 Wing, among the fighters they encountered near Rheine were at least five Me 262s. One of these was shot down by Capt Kåare Bolstad of No 332 Sqn for his second victory. It also proved to be the only jet shot down by a Norwegian pilot. A little over a week later, on 23 January, further heavy fighting with the Luftwaffe resulted in a rich harvest of jet claims for 2nd TAF units. During a mid-morning sweep by No 401 Sqn, its CO, and ace, Sqn Ldr Bill Klersy was leading his unit over an airfield north of Osnabrück when he spotted jets taking off from nearby Bramsche. Initially identified as Me 262s, the Spitfire pilots dived to attack, as the squadron diarist noted;

'Such a target is not very often seen, so after broadcasting the news to any other squadrons that happened to be in the vicinity, they immediately attacked. When the smoke had cleared and the squadron had returned to base to tally up the score, they found that three Me 262s had been destroyed and six damaged. One jet job crashed while trying to take off, so this was also claimed as a damaged.'

In fact the jets were Ar 234s of III./KG 76, and those destroyed fell to Flg Off Don Church for his third victory, Flg Off William 'Bud' Connell for his fourth success and Flg Off G A Hardy for his only aerial kill. Three others were damaged, including one by the CO. No 401 Sqn then strafed the airfield, claiming five Arado bombers damaged, with five-victory ace Flt Lt Frederick Murray claiming two and one shared.

Whilst this mayhem was happening Tempest Vs from No 56 Sqn were out on patrol, and near Achmer Flt Lt Frank MacLeod and Flg Off Ron Dennis came across an Me 262 at low level that they shot down. The former described the first of his four victories;

'We kept slightly below the Hun – the enemy aircraft was jinking slightly and we took advantage of this to close the range. The enemy aircraft was identified as an Me 262. The latter made a gentle turn to port, giving us an immediate advantage, and by cutting across the turn we closed to 150 yards. I fired a short burst with an angle off of approximately 30 degrees to port with no apparent effect. Still turning slightly with the Me 262, I increased deflection to about 40 degrees and fired, observing strikes immediately – I held my fire for about three seconds. My strikes were on the centre of the fuselage and on the tail unit – I saw flames and ceased firing. I broke away and next observed the enemy aircraft attempting to make a forced landing, with the fuselage and starboard jet on fire. He overshot the field in which it appeared he was going to land. After his tail unit had hit the ground the aircraft lifted and nosed into the next field, where it exploded.'

Shortly afterwards Spitfires of No 411 Sqn flew an armed reconnaissance towards Lingen and Münster. At 1215 hrs Flt Lt Dick Audet attacked

The only Norwegian pilot to shoot down a jet was Capt Kåare Bolstad of No 332 Sqn, who destroyed an Me 262 on 14 January. He was promoted to command his squadron soon afterwards, but on 3 April he was shot down by flak and killed whilst strafing near Zwolle, in Holland (*Bengt Stangvik*)

On 23 January 1945, whilst at the controls of ML141/YO-E, Flg Off Don Church of No 401 Sqn was on a sweep when he spotted jets taking off from Bramsche. They turned out to be Ar 234s of III./KG 76, and diving in, Church sent one of the aeroplanes crashing to its destruction for his fifth claim, three of which were destroyed. Seen here taxiing out at B88 Heesch in March 1945, ML141 fell victim to light flak on 25 April – its pilot bailed out (*PAC*)

During a remarkable sortie on 23 January 1945 No 411 Sqn ace Flt Lt Dick Audet shot down an Me 262 (for his his 11th, and last, victory) and damaged another on the ground when he strafed Rheine airfield. He caught another Me 262 in the air the next day at Münster and damaged it too *(DND)*

Audet's aircraft when he made his jet claims was Spitfire IX RR201, although it may have been coded DB-G at the time – the fighter was later recoded DB-R *(PAC)*

Rheine airfield, where, on a single pass, he strafed and destroyed an Me 262. Minutes later he spotted a jet in the air a few miles north of Rheine, and promptly shot it down. His victim is believed to have been Unteroffizier Kubizek of 4./KG(J) 51, and his demise provided Audet with his 11th, and last, victory. The following morning (24 January), near Münster, he damaged another Me 262.

Almost three weeks would pass before another German jet was engaged in the air, this time by ace Sqn Ldr David Fairbanks, the newly appointed CO of No 274 Sqn. He was leading a flight of eight Tempest Vs on an armed reconnaissance when he spotted a jet and chased it through the scattered clouds for more than 20 miles;

'I came through a small patch of cloud and saw the enemy aircraft about 800 yards dead ahead at approximately 1500 ft over Rheine airfield. He was just dropping his nose wheel and started to turn to starboard. I dropped my tanks on seeing the airfield and closed to approximately 250-300 yards and placed my bead on his starboard turbo [engine] and slightly above, firing a half-second burst to test my deflection. The enemy aircraft went straight down immediately and blew up in the centre of Rheine airfield.'

Although initially identified as an Me 262, his victim was in fact an Ar 234B of reconnaissance unit 1(F)/123, the jet being flown by Hauptmann Hans Felden. The next successes against jets were not long in coming.

On 14 February a No 416 Sqn patrol spotted eight Me 262s escorting an Ar 234, but as the unit diary wistfully stated, 'they proved bashful and the enemy pilots opened up the burners and pulled away into cloud cover'. However, others were more fortunate, as early in the morning, attracted by covering fighters over Rheine, the formidable Griffon-engined Spitfire XIVs of No 41 Sqn had their first engagement with Me 262s when, diving through the covering Fw 190Ds, Flg Off Eric Gray and WO Vivian Rossow each damaged a jet.

A significant number of Me 262s had been on sorties that day, their pilots being tasked with attacking Allied troops advancing on the heavily fortified Siegfried Line along the Dutch-German border. Two of these aircraft (from 5./KG(J) 51) were shot down by No 439 Sqn pilots Flt Lt Lyle Shaver and Flg Off Hugh Fraser in their Typhoons for their third and fourth victories, respectively. Fraser brought down Feldwebel Werner Witzmann, while Shaver's Me 262 was being flown by Oberleutnant Hans-Georg Richter. Within minutes Capt Freddie Green of No 184 Sqn, in another Typhoon, spotted a pair of jets near Arnhem

and, finding himself astern of one of them, was able to open fire and damage it. This was the first claim made by a South African Air Force pilot against a jet.

Then, shortly before dusk, Australian ace Flt Lt Tony Gaze was flying a Spitfire XIV of No 610 Sqn over the German town of Kleve, on the Dutch border, when he saw some jets. After unsuccessfully chasing several Ar 234s, he spotted three Me 262s;

Australian ace Flt Lt Tony Gaze, flying Spitfire XIVs with No 41 Sqn, destroyed an Me 262 on 14 February and shared in the destruction of an Ar 234 on 12 April. In the closing days of the war he also briefly saw an He 162 in formation with an Me 262 (*Tony Gaze*)

'I dived down behind them and closed in, crossing behind the formation, and attacked the port aircraft which was lagging slightly. I could not see my sight properly as we were flying straight into the sun, but fired from dead astern, at a range of 350 yards, hitting it in the starboard jet [engine] with the second burst – at which point the other two aircraft immediately dived into cloud. It pulled up slowly and turned to starboard and I fired, obtaining more strikes on the fuselage and jet, which caught fire. The enemy aircraft rolled over onto its back and dived through cloud. I turned 180 [degrees] and dived after it, calling on the R/T to warn my No 2. On breaking cloud I saw an aircraft hit the ground and explode about a mile ahead of me.'

The first jet shot down by a Griffon-engined Spitfire was an Me 262A of 3./KG(J) 51 flown by Feldwebel Rudolf Hoffmann, who was killed.

There were several more encounters with jets for 2nd TAF fighters during the rest of February, although these only resulted in several 'damaged' claims. Fighter Command's Mustang-equipped long-range escort units were also occasionally encountering jets whilst escorting daylight raids by Bomber Command. On 21 February Flg Off Jan Borowczyk of No 315 Sqn reported spotting what was almost certainly an Me 163;

'I caught sight of a single strange looking German aircraft proceeding to the east at about 15,000 to 16,000 ft. He did not see me yet and my heart jumped when I realised that this was probably the new German jet fighter ME 163, which I saw below. All I could think of now was what it would mean if I managed to shoot down the first of these planes to add to the high reputation of my Squadron. Thinking this way, I gathered all the speed I could, attempting to close up and to fall unexpectedly on the German. Alas, the German pilot was alert enough to spot an enemy fighter hurtling down in his direction. I was still at least some 1500 ft away from him when his aircraft gave off a puff of white smoke and started to move away with astounding acceleration.'

The first big encounter between Fighter Command Mustang IIIs and German jets came on 23 March when an attack by 100 Lancasters on Bremen was intercepted by around 20 Me 262s. Southwest of the target, Flg Off Albert Yeardley, who had only recently joined No 126 Sqn, put a well-aimed burst into one and the Me 262 went straight in, giving him credit for the first jet shot down by an RAF Mustang – this was also Yeardley's third, and last, victory. Also engaged was No 118 Sqn, led by

On 9 April Flt Sgt Toni Murkowski was part of a bomber escort to Hamburg when No 309 Sqn engaged a group of Me 262s. He duly claimed one of the four jets that were shot down, which were amongst the final Polish victories of the war – he also damaged a second jet (*Toni Murkowski*)

Toni Murkowski was flying Mustang III FB385/WC-W over Hamburg when he achieved his jet victory on 9 April (*Toni Murkowski*)

Flt Lt Paddy Harbison, and he claimed one damaged, as did five-victory ace Flt Lt Mike Giddings;

'As we turned to rejoin the bombers I dived on another ME 262, which was turning below me, and I fired a two- to three-second burst from 700 down 500 yards, seeing a couple of strikes and part of the starboard wing root fly off. It was impossible to close the range to these attackers.'

Giddings, who later became Air Marshal Sir Michael Giddings, fired 60 rounds from his four guns.

Over the next few weeks the escort fighters engaged jets on a regular basis, and on the 31st more were encountered near Hamburg. This time they could not be caught, however, as Flg Off Bill Fleming of No 154 Sqn recalled;

'South of the target I noticed some vapour trails several thousand feet above us going down in the same direction. Shortly afterwards I observed several Me 262s diving through our formation from above and behind, travelling at high speed. We dropped our tanks and dived on the 262s, but before getting within range they opened fire on the leading bombers with what looked like rocket projectiles and cannon, scoring hits on at least two of the bombers. One of the 262s, breaking away from the attack, came back under us at high speed. We opened fire at extreme range before he pulled away with his superior speed.'

Albert Yeardley was more successful and damaged one of them.

However, things improved on 9 April during another raid on Hamburg when Polish No 133 Wing, led by six-victory ace Wg Cdr Kazimierz Rutkowski, shot down four. Sqn Ldr Józef Żulikowski, CO of No 306 Sqn, shot down one 15 miles west of the target for his third, and final, victory, whilst Flt Lt Mieczysław Gorzula and Flt Lt Jerzy Mencel of No 309 Sqn claimed an Me 262 each. A fourth fell to No 309 Sqn's Flt Sgt Toni Murkowski, who also damaged another. He told Andrew Thomas;

'During this raid on Hamburg we were off on the right, and suddenly the jets appeared from behind. I was in a turn and managed to slip behind one – gaining in speed, I opened up when I got to within 200 yards behind a jet. I could see bits flying off the engine and perhaps the flaps came off and he just dived in from about 20,000+ ft. I then caught another. The 262s were much faster than the Mustang, and if they had just gone straight I'd never have caught them. I later met an air gunner from one of the Lancasters who showed me a photo of a Mustang diving through the bombers, and when we compared log books it was of me chasing the first 262!'

The following afternoon 200 Lancasters attacked Leipzig, and as the pathfinder indicators went down a No 405 Sqn Lancaster flown by Sqn Ldr Campbell Mussells was attacked by a Komet, whose fire shot

During the final months of the war in Europe the Mosquito VI intruders of the Fighter Experimental Flight patrolled enemy airfields at night from their airfield at Wittering. Flying TA386/ZQ-F on 22 March 1945, New Zealand intruder ace Flg Off Roy Lelong damaged three Me 262s parked at Neuburg airfield. TA386 survived only a matter of weeks after VE Day, the Mosquito being damaged beyond repair when it swung on takeoff and lost its undercarriage in an accident at Y9 Dijon on 19 June 1945 (*Robert Forsyth collection*)

away the rear turret and caused other damage. Pilots of several Mustang squadrons reported sighting Me 163s, and Flg Off John 'Slops' Haslope of No 165 Sqn spotted the rocket fighter that attacked Mussells' aircraft. He 'firewalled' his throttle and dived after it;

'I noticed a bomber begin to smoke and something appeared to fly off it. This resolved itself into an Me 163, which climbed vertically at great speed. The Me 163 turned towards me and I had a shot at him in a right hand turn, range about 900 yards and 30 degrees' deflection, but observed no strikes. The Me 163 then spiralled into a vertical dive, which I followed, firing several bursts of about two to three seconds, observing strikes on four occasions on the wing roots and several small pieces came off. The Me 163 continued on down and was observed to hit the ground and explode.'

The tactical fighters based on the Continent also continued to see action against Luftwaffe jets through March as Allied troops closed on the Rhine. During an early patrol on the 2nd Flt Lt Danny Reid of No 41 Sqn caught an Ar 234 near Nijmegen in his Spitfire XIV;

'I closed to 100 yards or less, firing with 0.50-in machine guns and cannon whilst still overtaking. I saw strikes on the port wing, jet engine and fuselage. I continued firing and saw flashes in the smoke, breaking away and being hit in the port radiator by debris. I next saw the enemy aircraft going down in a wide spiral, with white smoke pouring from holes all along the port wing, and dark smoke from the fuselage. A large piece of the enemy aircraft suddenly flew off, and one person bailed out, parachute opening. The enemy aircraft steepened its dive and crashed somewhere near Enschede.'

Soon afterwards a Tempest V patrol from No 222 Sqn spotted a pair of Ar 234s, as Flt Lt George Varley described;

'I dived and turned to port, closing to 1000 yards before firing a one-second burst with ten-degree deflection. Looking down and around, I saw another jet plane flying below in the other direction. I closed to 200 yards and fired a two-second burst dead astern, and a huge explosion with red flame occurred.'

Varley's victim was a jet from 9./KG 76 flown by Leutnant Eberhard Rogle, whilst the other aircraft he fired on and claimed as damaged in fact crash-landed and was written off. Varley

The first of only two Me 163s shot down by an RAF aircraft fell on 10 April 1945 to Flg Off John 'Slops' Haslope, who was flying a Mustang from No 165 Sqn at the time (*Chris Goss collection*)

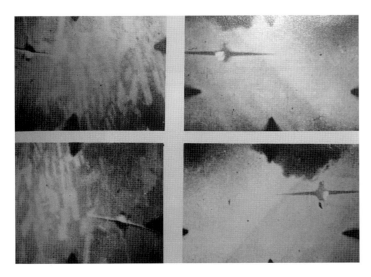

Four frames taken from the gun camera film exposed by 'Slops' Haslope when he downed his Me 163 on 10 April. The Komet proved to be Haslope's only aerial success (*No 165 Sqn Records*)

ended the war with four victories to his name.

On 12 March Flt Lt Len Watt of No 401 Sqn claimed his first victory when, on a patrol over the Rhine, he spotted an Me 262 at 2500 ft just west of Wesel. Positioning himself astern of the jet, he fired two bursts and saw it 'issue smoke and go down'. His victory was later confirmed. The following day Flg Off Howard Nicholson claimed the first jet victory credited to Spitfire XIV-equipped No 402 Sqn when he shot down an Ar 234, another of which fell to No 222 Sqn Tempest Vs on the 14th.

It was almost a month before the next 2nd TAF jet victory. On 10 April Flt Lt Tony Gaze, now with No 41 Sqn, chased an Ar 234 but the jet outpaced him and he then had to avoid a patrol of Fw 190s. However, two days, later he had better luck when on patrol with Flt Lt Derek Rake, who recounted the highlights of the mission to Andrew Thomas;

'Tony was leading the flight. We came out on top at around 20,000 ft, and as we levelled out, I recall seeing what I recognised as an Arado 234 twin jet break cloud to port ahead of us and below. I was in the near perfect position for a quarter attack. My Spit, a XIVE, was fitted with a gyro gunsight with a ranging twist grip on the throttle. As I dived towards the target I was able to position the jet within the diamond markers on the gunsight, thus having the correct range and deflection to open fire. My opening burst hit the starboard engine and it was smoking as it rolled over and dived towards the cloud. I got in one or two more bursts as I followed it down. I believe that I claimed the "kill", but I think that Tony must have had a share in finishing it off.'

Jet victories were then regularly claimed, and on 14 April No 41 Sqn's ace CO Sqn Ldr John Shepherd was near Nordholz airfield when he spotted two aircraft;

'I recognised them as an ME 163 being towed by a ME 110. I was closing very rapidly but managed to get a short burst in on the ME 110, obtaining strikes on the port engine and cockpit. The 110 went into a left-hand diving turn, turned over on to its back and crashed into a field, bursting into flames. The 163 appeared to break away from the 110 and make a wide left-hand turn, finally diving straight in about three fields away from the 110.'

Shepherd was credited with both destroyed. The following day Flt Lts Jim McCairns and Neill Cox of No 56 Sqn were patrolling over the rapidly shrinking area of enemy-held territory when, north of Hamburg, they spotted a jet that they identified as an Me 262, but which was in fact an Ar 234, taking off from Kaltenkirchen. Cox's Combat Report for the subsequent action, which gave him ace status, read as follows;

'After Yellow Leader's last attack, the enemy aircraft was making a gradual turn to port and I closed in astern to 200 yards, closing to 75 yards and firing all the time, allowing five-ten degrees of deflection. I saw strikes on the fuselage, wing roots and starboard power unit. The enemy aircraft began to turn more steeply, before striking a house and bursting into flames.'

On 17 April, in a solo attack on Ludwigslust, No 401 Sqn's Flt Lt Johnny MacKay attacked aircraft in the face of heavy flak and damaged three Ar 234s. Two days later over Schleswig-Holstein during an armed reconnaissance, Flt Lt Tony Gaze's section chased an Me 262 that was apparently leading what they initially identified as a V1 flying bomb 'in formation'. However, it was subsequently assessed that this was probably one of the new He 162s that were based at Leck, making it one of the very few encounters that the RAF had with the *Volksjäger*. That same day, in the same area, No 222 Sqn almost certainly engaged another He 162, as Flt Lt Geoffrey Walkington described;

'I immediately broke off my attack on the airfield and chased this aircraft, which was camouflaged mottled green with a yellow underside and appeared to have twin fins and rudders and one engine. The nose of the aircraft had a drooping appearance and the wings (plan view) resembled those of a Me 109. Due to my loss of speed on turning, the enemy aircraft pulled away to about 1500 yards. Having now recognised this aircraft as hostile by its camouflage, I gave chase, but was unable to close, my IAS [indicated airspeed] being 350 mph. The enemy aircraft did a 360-degree turn to starboard, which I followed, turning inside. During my turn I managed to close to 1000 yards.

'Being unable to gain further I trimmed my aircraft carefully, and allowing about three-quarters of a ring above the enemy aircraft, I fired short bursts. The enemy aircraft then pulled up through cloud, which was eight-tenths at 3000 ft. I followed through a gap and passed the enemy aircraft spinning down out of control from about 3500 ft. I then watched the enemy aircraft explode on the ground near Husum aerodrome. The enemy aircraft burned for about 30 seconds, emitting flames and thick black smoke, which, however, ceased completely at the end of the period. Claim one unidentified enemy aircraft destroyed.'

German accounts concur with this report, and it is possible that Walkington's victim was Fahnenjunker-Feldwebel Günther Kirchner of I./JG 1.

By now Allied fighters were roaming at will over the shrinking Reich, and on 25 April No 41 Sqn's Spitfire XIVs and No 486 Sqn's Tempest Vs attacked Lübeck. No 41 Sqn's Flt Lt Peter Cowell caught some Me 262s over the Ratzenburger See, shooting one down and damaging a second. Unusually, No 486 Sqn's section was attacked by some Me 262s, but the pilots involved soon turned the tables and gave chase after the jets. Approaching Lübeck, V1 ace Flg Off Keith Smith finally got his chance;

'I went down to attack and observed the 262 to have its wheels down. The enemy aircraft spotted me and broke sharply to port. I opened fire from 800 yards with two rings deflection, and following in the turn held my

Tempest V pilot Flg Off Geoffrey Walkington of No 222 Sqn (right) claimed 'one unidentified enemy aircraft destroyed' that he described as having 'twin fins and rudders and one engine' over Husum on 19 April 1945. It is possible that his victim was Fahnenjunker-Feldwebel Günther Kirchner of 3./JG 1. If this was indeed the case, Walkington had shot down the only He 162 credited to the Allies (*Chris Thomas collection*)

High-scoring ace Wg Cdr James 'Eddie' Edwards was leading No 127 Wing in his personal Spitfire XVI (TD147/JFE) on 29 April 1945 when he damaged an Fw 190 and an Me 262 (*J F Edwards*)

fire down to zero yards. I overshot, pulled up sharply and came down on him, opening fire from 400 yards with a half-ring deflection. The 262 was now at 50 ft over the runway. As it touched down I saw the starboard wing touch the runway and white smoke coming from the starboard unit. It slewed to starboard, and as I climbed away I saw smoke rising up to 200 ft and flames coming from the 262, which was now about 100 yards off the runway.'

Flt Lt Bill Stowe of Spitfire XIV-equipped No 130 Sqn also strafed an Me 262 as it lifted off from Lübeck, and the pilot bailed out as it crashed. He was only awarded a probable, however, although he 'made ace' on 30 April.

On 26 April Bremen fell, and that same day a section of No 263 Sqn's Typhoons were bounced by Me 262s as they were landing at B111 Ahlhorn. The remaining fighters from the unit duly attacked one of the jets and brought it down. On the 29th the 21st Army Group crossed the Elbe with relative ease, and during the day one of the leading Canadian aces of World War 2 returned to action. Leading No 127 Wing, Wg Cdr James 'Eddie' Edwards was west of Hamburg when, as was described in his biography, 'An aircraft popped out of a cloud. This time it was a brand new, and deadly, Messerschmitt 262 jet. As he was travelling very fast the Spitfires had no chance of catching him, so Eddie and his wingman fired at long range and saw hits on the fuselage. The jet kept going and disappeared into a cloud. The next day he got shots off at another Me 262, but it climbed away from them and easily escaped.'

There was possibly one more encounter with jets during April, for on the 30th Leutnant Hans Rechenberg of II./JG 1 reported that he was shot at by a Spitfire while ferrying an He 162 from Rostock to Leck, forcing him to crash-land his *Volksjager* near Wismar. It is uncertain who shot him down, but it is possible that it may have been a pilot from No 412 Sqn, who claimed several Bf 109s in the same general area that evening.

By the beginning of May the Third Reich was almost finished, and on the evening of the 2nd Plt Off Des Watkins of the Belgian-manned No 350 Sqn was leading six Spitfire XIVs over Schleswig-Holstein when, west of Keil, they spotted an Ar 234 approaching Hohn airfield. The Welshman described how he became an ace;

'I saw in the circuit of Hohn aerodrome a jet aircraft, which I identified as an Arado 234, going in to land. I dived from 8000 ft followed by the rest of the section, closed to within 50 yards behind the enemy aircraft and sprayed the mainplane and side of the fuselage with machine gun fire. I broke away to port as I saw the aircraft smoking.'

Others in Watkins' section then finished off the last German jet to fall to the guns of the 'King's Men', who, in all, had been credited with 37 jets destroyed. Of the pilots to make claims against a jet, 29 of them were aces.

CHAPTER SEVEN

SOVIET VICTORIES

Due to the simple fact that most of the Luftwaffe's jets were used to combat the Allied aerial onslaught in the West, fighter pilots of the Red Army Air Force (*Voenno-Vozdushniye Sily Krasnoy Armii*, VVS KA) in the East had scant opportunities to engage such aircraft until the Red Army began to close in on central Germany. Because of the sheer number of jets shot down by the USAAF and RAF, history has lost sight of the fact that a handful of Soviet pilots, several of them aces, downed at least five Me 262s and Ar 234s in the closing months of the war.

The first Soviet pilot to do so was Maj Ivan Kozhedub, the leading Allied ace with 62 confirmed victories and three times a Hero of the Soviet Union (HSU). He was serving with the 176th Guards Fighter Aviation Regiment (*Gvardveyskiy Istrebitelniy Aviapolk*, or GIAP) at the time of his success against the Me 262, having joined the Lavochkin La-7-equipped unit on 21 August 1944 upon its creation. By this late stage in the war Kozhedub had received two HSU awards and been credited with 48 aerial victories. In this unit each pilot was assigned his own aircraft and would fly with the same wingman. Kozhedub's new wingman was Maj Dmitrii Titarenko, who would end the war with 23 victories to his name.

On 19 February 1945, Kozhedub and Titarenko were patrolling an area south of Frankfurt at 10,000 ft when they spotted an unidentified aircraft flying in the opposite direction down the River Oder. Many years later, Kozhedub recalled;

The first Soviet pilot to shoot down a jet was Maj Ivan Kozhedub, the leading Allied ace with 62 confirmed victories and three times a Hero of the Soviet Union. He was serving with the La-7-equipped 176th GIAP when he claimed an Me 262 shot down south of Frankfurt. Kozhedub's victim, Unteroffizier Kurt Lange of 1./KG(J) 54, was killed when his fighter literally disintegrated in mid-air after being hit by 20 mm cannon rounds (*Gennady Petrov collection*)

Lt Gen Yevgenii Savitskii, shown here standing in the cockpit of a Yak-7, was the highest ranking Allied pilot to claim a jet victory in World War 2. In late-March 1945, 34-year-old Savitskii, known as 'Drakon', engaged an unidentified twin-engined aircraft and fired several bursts before it escaped. The aeroplane was later identified as an Me 262, and Savitskii was credited with its destruction. He finished the war with 22 individual and two shared victories, making him the most successful general officer of the Soviet forces in aerial combat (*Gennady Petrov collection*)

'Titarenko and I were on a "lone wolf" south of Frankfurt when I noticed an aeroplane below us at an altitude of 350 metres [2170 ft]. It was flying along the Oder at a speed that was marginal for my La-7 to match. Nevertheless, I made a quick "about-face" and started pursuing it at full throttle, coming down so as to approach it from under its "belly". My wingman opened fire, and the Me 262 began turning to the left, over to my side, losing speed in the process. That was the end of it. I would never have overtaken it if it had flown in a straight line. The main thing was to attack enemy aeroplanes during turns, climbs or dives, and not to lose precious seconds chasing them.'

Kozhedub had closed to within 500 yards of his unsuspecting victim, Unteroffizier Kurt Lange of 1./KG(J) 54, and was just about to open fire with his 20 mm cannon when he saw green tracer rounds flying past the Me 262. Titarenko had seemingly spoiled Kozhedub's chances of claiming a rare victory over a German jet by firing too early. As the Soviet ace subsequently related, the enemy pilot, now fully aware that he was under attack, broke left towards Kozhedub, who fired a highly accurate burst that caused the jet to disintegrate in mid-air. Lange did not survive the encounter, which gave Ivan Kozhedub his 58th aerial success.

Just over a month after Kozhedub's victory, on 22 March, Lt L I Sivko, a non-ace with Yakovlev Yak-9-equipped 812nd IAP, shot down an Me 262 that was attacking an Ilyushin Il-2m3 *Shturmovik*. Minutes later Sivko in turn fell victim to another Me 262 from 10./JG 7, the latter possibly being flown by high-scoring jet ace Oberleutnant Franz Schall – 16 of his 133 victories were claimed in the Me 262.

As the Red Army closed in on Berlin, the situation presented many VVS-KA units with the opportunity to occasionally engage jets. Amongst the successful pilots was Lt Gen Yevgenii Savitskii, who was the highest ranking Allied pilot to claim a jet victory. By mid-1944 he had risen to the rank of lieutenant general and been placed in command of the 3rd Fighter Aviation Corps (*Istrebitelniy Aviakorpus*), which included more than 200 fighters – mainly Yak-1Ms.

In November 1944, Savitskii's corps was withdrawn from the front for conversion to the Yak-3. Once this had been completed his unit was redeployed and attached to the 16th Air Army (*Vozdushnaya Armiya*) for the assault on Germany, which began in January 1945. The following month Savitskii and Maj P Okolenov engaged a lone Me 262 without success. In late March Savitskii spotted an unidentified twin-engined aircraft flying at very high speed, and he managed to fire several ineffective bursts before it escaped. The aircraft was later identified as a Me 262, and despite stating that he was unsure whether he had hit the aeroplane or not, Savitskii was given credit for shooting it down. He ended the war with a final score of 22 individual and two shared victories, making him the most successful general officer of the Soviet forces in aerial combat.

A combat veteran, and ace, from the Khalkin Gol border clashes with Japan in the summer of 1939 and the Winter War in Finland later that same year, Maj Arsenii Vorozheikin engaged an Ar 234 over Berlin in mid-April 1945. The pall of smoke that hung over much of the German capital at this time prevented the Soviet ace from seeing the jet crash, and the victory, one of his last of the war, was not officially credited. Vorozheikin's final tally totalled 63 victories in three wars (including 13 shared), of which 46 were claimed in World War 2 (*Gennady Petrov collection*)

Maj Arsenii Vorozheikin had the unique distinction of engaging an Ar 234 during the final weeks of the war in Europe, the high-scoring pre-war ace serving with the Yak-3-equipped 7th Guards Fighter Aviation Division at the time. A veteran of combat against the Japanese in the Khalkin Gol border clashes in the summer of 1939 and the Winter War in Finland later that same year, Vorozheikin had claimed 46 individual victories in five years of combat by the time he joined Frontal Aviation (*Frontovoi Aviapolk*) as its senior inspector pilot for combat preparedness in the autumn of 1944. This role allowed him to fly on a number of fronts, imparting his hard-won knowledge of aerial combat to young Soviet pilots.

Whilst working with units assigned to the Yak-3-equipped 7th GIAD in mid-April 1945, Vorozheikin was over Berlin when he bounced an Ar 234. The pall of smoke that hung over much of the German capital at this time prevented the Soviet ace from seeing the jet crash, and the victory, one of his last of the war, was not officially credited. Vorozheikin's final tally totalled 63 victories in three wars (including 13 shared), of which 46 were claimed in World War 2.

On 27 April both JG 7 and JV 44 launched a number of sorties, and after downing a handful of P-47s, several pilots headed east. Here, they sighted a column of Soviet trucks, claiming 65 destroyed in strafing attacks. Shortly thereafter, a group of 20+ Il-2 *Shturmoviks* where spotted and attacked. The JG 7 pilots claimed six Il-2s destroyed for the loss of two of their own. The next day, Leutnant Ernst-Rudolf Geldmacher of 11./JG 7 was shot down and killed while taking off from Prague-Ruzyne. Although it is impossible to determine with any certainty, Geldmacher may have fallen to Yak-3 pilot Snr Lt Garri Merkvaladze of the 152nd GIAP. He finished the war with 15 victories (two shared) to his name. On the last day of April, ten-victory ace Snr Lt Ivan Kuznetsov of the 107th GIAP claimed an Me 262 destroyed – the last known jet claim made by a Soviet pilot. German records indicate that I./KG(J) 54 lost an Me 262A-2a and its pilot on this date, although it was listed as having fallen to Red Army anti-aircraft fire.

APPENDICES

COLOUR PLATES

1

P-38J-15 42-104425 *BOOMERANG* of Capt Arthur Jeffrey, 434th FS/479th FG, Wattisham, July 1944

On 28 July 1944, the 479th FG was providing withdrawal support for a group of B-17s when 'Newcross Yellow' Flight leader Capt Arthur F Jeffrey of the 434th FS noticed that B-17G 42-107997 *She Hasta* was steadily falling behind the formation. When the bomber was attacked from 'five o'clock' by a Me 163, Jeffrey engaged the rocket fighter and scored many hits. The Komet, with the P-38 pilot in pursuit, went into a vertical dive that saw its speed easily exceed 500 mph. Jeffrey pulled out at the last possible moment, but the Me 163 was last seen entering a solid undercast at around 3000 ft still in a vertical dive doing an estimated 600 mph. The Komet was Jeffrey's second of four P-38 victories, and he would go on to score ten victories in the P-51. His Me 163 was the only jet/rocket-powered aircraft to fall to a P-38.

2

P-47D-28 44-19713 *Miss Pussy "IV"* of Capt Valmore Beaudrault, 386th FS/365th FG, A68 Juvincourt, Belgium, October 1944

Despite the Mustang taking over as the USAAF's premier fighter in the ETO from the summer of 1944 up to VE Day, the first three Me 262s downed by USAAF fighters fell to Thunderbolts. On 2 October 1944, 21-year-old Capt Valmore J Beaudrault was leading a flight of P-47s that was bounced by a Me 262. After a chase in and out of clouds, Beaudrault entered a low-level scissors engagement with Oberfeldwebel Hieronymous Lauer from 3./KG 51 until the wingtip of his Me 262 struck the ground, sending it into a fiery cartwheel. This was the first jet to be shot down by a Ninth Air Force fighter.

3

P-51D-10 44-14164 *DETROIT Miss* of 1Lt Urban 'Ben' Drew, 375th FS/361st FG, Little Walden, October 1944

In mid-September 1944, 1Lt Urban 'Ben' Drew had his first encounter with an Me 262 near Hamm, in Germany. Although his Mustang hit 500 mph in the dive from 20,000 ft, Drew could not close on the jet in order to open fire. On 7 October the 361st FG was near Achmer when Drew spotted two Me 262s taking off. Diving on the pair of jets from 15,000 ft, and with flak exploding all around him, he fired a burst that caused the first jet to explode directly in front of him – Drew flew straight on right through the fireball. The second jet broke to the left, and Drew racked his Mustang into a 6G turn at 400 mph. As his vision began to fade Drew opened fire and 'walked' his tracer rounds up the fuselage until they slammed into the cockpit, shattering the canopy and sending the jet down in an inverted spin. In less than 60 seconds

Drew had shot down two jet fighters, becoming the first of only two USAAF pilots to achieve the feat. At A84 Chièvres, in Belgium, on 4 April 1945, 44-14164 was subsequently written off in a wheels-up belly landing, the fighter having suffered engine failure in flight.

4

P-47D-28 42-28442 of 2Lt Huie Lamb, 82nd FS/78th FG, Duxford, October 1944

On 15 October 1944 2Lt Huie Lamb, flying as wingman to Capt John I Brown, spotted an Me 262 near Hanover. Unable to acquire the jet himself, Brown gave Lamb permission to attack it. Lamb activated his fighter's water injection in the dive, and the P-47 was indicating 525 mph when he levelled out at an altitude of just 100 ft. His opponent, Fahnenjunker-Feldwebel Edgar Junghans of I./KG 51, made a hard left turn in an attempt to drag Lamb over a nearby airfield in the hope that defending flak batteries would shoot the pursuing American down. Although Lamb's P-47 did indeed take a number of hits, he stuck to the Me 262 long enough to fire a telling burst into its left engine, which sent it crashing into the ground. Although Lamb never 'made ace', on 19 March 1945 he received a half credit for the destruction of an Ar 234, making him one of just 13 USAAF pilots to score multiple jet kills.

5

P-51D-5 44-13317 of Capt Freddie Glover, 336th FS/4th FG, Debden, November 1944

By early November 1944, seven USAAF fighter groups had claimed 12 German jets, but the 4th FG, the famed Debden 'Eagles', was not among them. On 2 November, however, ace Capt Freddie Glover shot down an Me 163 from 2./JG 400 with a quick burst from 400 yards. On that day Glover was flying Capt Donald Emerson's Mustang, which had originally boasted 'Donald Duck' nose art as seen here. By the time of Glover's victory over the Komet it is likely that the famous nose art had been removed, so 44-13317 is depicted here as it appeared when Glover flew the fighter in August 1944. The Mustang was lost on 18 March 1945 when it suffered engine failure and crashed east of Fordham, Cambridgeshire, the pilot successfully bailing out.

6

P-51D-15 44-15028 *Red Dog* of Capt Louis Norley, 335th FS/4th FG, Debden, November 1944

Moments after Capt Glover downed his Komet, fellow ace Capt Louis Norley latched onto another Me 163 that was not using its rocket motor and quickly overshot the fighter. He pulled up and closed in for another attack just as the pilot, Oberfeldwebel Jakob Bollenrath of 1./

JG 400, belatedly ignited the rocket motor. Norley fired several bursts and saw strikes on the tail that caused the Komet to roll over and crash into a village, the aircraft exploding on impact with the ground. Subsequently 44-15028 was passed on to the 359th FS/356th FG.

7

P-51D-5 44-11161 *June Nite* of Capt Ernest Fiebelkorn, 77th FS/20th FG, Kings Cliffe, November 1944

On 8 November 1944 Capt Ernest Fiebelkorn was leading 'Yellow' Flight near Lake Dummer when he spotted an Me 262 and then chased it at low altitude until a pair of P-51s from the 364th FS/357th FG cut him off as the jet turned and began to climb towards the clouds. Moments later it came spinning out of the clouds and crashed, taking the life of high-scoring ace Major Walter Nowotny. Although Fiebelkorn never fired on Nowotny's jet, he shared credit in the downing of the Me 262 with 1Lt Edward Haydon of the 357th FG. This was Fiebelkorn's ninth, and final, victory of the war. Subsequently assigned to the 20th FG's 55th FS, 44-11161 was destroyed when it crashed on take-off from Kings Cliffe on 13 June 1945.

8

P-51D-44-15041 *PETIE 3RD* of Lt Col John Meyer, 487th FS/352nd FG, Y29 Asch, Belgium, December 1944

On 31 December 1944, the day before he scored his 24th and 25th victories, 352nd FG deputy CO Lt Col John Meyer was leading the 328th FS on a patrol (in his assigned Mustang, which was maintained by the 487th FS) when an Ar 234 was detected by fighter controllers on radar. This aeroplane was duly damaged by future jet killer Capt Donald Bryan before he broke off his attack when Meyer spotted a second Arado bomber closing on the tail of the pursuing Mustang. Meyer chased the second Ar 234 without success, before eventually firing on a third Arado. Even though he observed no hits, Meyer claimed, and was awarded, credit for downing the first Ar 234 to fall to the USAAF.

9

P-51D-15 44-15026 *CATHY MAE/ "KARGER'S DOLLIE"* of 1Lt Dale Karger, 364th FS/357th FG, Leiston, January 1945

By the middle of January 1945, the 357th FG had only scored 3.5 aerial victories over Luftwaffe jets. On the 20th of that month the 364th FS swept an area 50 miles southeast of Heilbronn, in Germany, after 3rd Air Division B-17s had hit railway marshalling yards. Near Munich 19-year-old 1Lt Dale Karger and his wingman chased an Me 262 and, using the K-14 gunsight, the future ace fired a burst from long range that shattered the jet's canopy, forcing the pilot to bail out. This was Karger's fifth victory, making him the youngest jet killer in the USAAF. He finished the war with 7.5 aerial victories. His mount on this occasion is unknown, for his assigned fighter, 44-15026, had been shot down by flak southwest of Paderborn on 10 January, killing 1Lt Fred McCall.

10

P-51D-15 44-15630 *JUNIOR MISS* of Capt James Browning, 363rd FS/357th FG, Leiston, February 1945

During the 9 February 1945 escort mission flown by the 357th FG, seven-victory ace Capt James Browning was at the controls of 44-15630, which was normally flown by 1Lt Glenwood Zarnke, rather than his assigned P-51D-15 44-14937. Near the village of Fulda, a flight of four Me 262s was called out below the Mustangs from the 363rd, and Browning dived on the jets. During the engagement he collided with the aircraft flown by Oberstleutnant Volprecht Freiherr von Riedesel, commander of KG(J) 54, and both aircraft crashed 60 miles east of the target area. No one in the squadron saw what happened and the details of Browning's fate remained a mystery for five decades.

11

P-51D-15 44-15422 of Capt Donald Bochkay, 363rd FS/357th FG, Leiston, February 1945

Capt Donald Bochkay was flying as wingman to Capt Browning on the 9 February mission that cost the latter his life. When Browning bounced the quartet of Me 262s Bochkay latched on to one and fired a well-aimed burst that caused the jet to slow considerably. He broke right to avoid colliding with the Me 262, which rolled over and went straight in. Bochkay heard Browning's last transmission that he was covering him, but he never saw his flight leader again. The jet was Bochkay's 13th aerial victory, and his final kill of the war was another Me 262, which he downed on 18 April 1945. Six days after Bochkay's first jet victory, 44-15422 was badly damaged in a wheels-up belly landing at Leiston when the fighter suffered engine failure.

12

P-51D-5 44-13818 *MAH IDEEL* of 2Lt Dudley Amoss, 38th FS/55th FG, Wormingford, February 1945

On 15 February 1945, Amoss was flying one of more than 500 fighters escorting bombers to oil industry targets. Spotting an Me 262 below his flight, Amoss dived on the jet and caught the German completely by surprise. His first burst struck the engines and the second, from just 200 yards astern of the fighter, caused it to explode. Despite this, somehow the pilot still managed to bail out. On 21 March, Amoss 'made ace' by destroying three Fw 190s, only to be shot down by flak near Hopsten airfield minutes later. He spent the rest of the war as a PoW. By then 44-13818 had been lost in action, the fighter crashing on 2 March near Limburg, in Germany. Its pilot, 2Lt Samuel Anderson, was killed.

13

La-7 'White 27' of Maj Ivan Kozhedub, 176th GIAP, Germany, February 1945

On 19 February 1945, Maj Ivan Kozhedub and his wingman were patrolling an area south of Frankfurt when they spotted an unidentified aircraft flying down the River Oder. As the pair turned in behind the fighter in their La-7s, they identified it as an Me 262. Kozhedub approached with stealth, but his wingman fired too early, which caused the jet's pilot to break to the left. Kozhedub opened fire with his 20 mm cannon, causing the jet to disintegrate in mid-air. This was Ivan Kozhedub's 55th of 62 aerial victories – a tally that made him the highest scoring Allied pilot of the war. His La-7 had been issued new to him in late 1944 as a replacement for another aircraft, and he kept it through to war's end. The fighter was saved for display post-war as part of the Victory against Fascism programme, which preserved historically significant weapons from World War 2. It has been displayed at the Central Air Force Museum at Monino Airfield, east of Moscow, for many years.

14

P-51K-5 44-11628 *Worra Bird 3/Bashful Betsy* of Capt Donald Bryan, 486th FS/352nd FG, A84 Chièvres, Belgium, March 1945

After coming away from three late-1944 engagements with the Ar 234 with just a single 'damaged' claim to his name, Capt Donald Bryan finally downed an Arado bomber flying Capt G A Middleton's P-51K 44-11628 (which had previously served with the 343rd FS/55th FG) on 14 March 1945. Spotting the aeroplane near the Ludendorff Bridge at Remagen, he fired almost all of his ammunition in an extended chase that only came to an end when both of the jet's engines began smoking. As they failed, the Ar 234 rolled over onto its back and Bryan saw the pilot jettison the canopy, but he did not get out. This victory brought Bryan's final wartime tally to 13.333, making him the second highest scorer in the 328th FS.

15

P-51D-15 44-15521 *SCREAMIN DEMON* of Capt Ray Wetmore, 370th FS/359th FG, East Wretham, March 1945

Following Capt Arthur Jeffrey's initial victory over the Me 163 on 29 July 1944, USAAF fighter pilots shot down a further four Komets. On 15 March 1945, the 359th FG was escorting a formation of bombers at 25,000 ft near Wittenberg when Capt Ray Wetmore spotted a pair of Me 163s 5000 ft below his section of Mustangs. As he attempted to bounce the rocket fighters, the German pilots saw his Mustang and pulled up into a 70-degree climb. They then nosed their aircraft over and headed for home in a steep dive that saw Wetmore push his Mustang to nearly 600 mph. He fired a number of bursts that blew half the left wing off one of the Komets, forcing the pilot to bail out. This was the final Me 163 to fall to USAAF guns. Having initially served with the 350th FS/353rd FG, 44-15521 was eventually written off on 7 September 1945 when it suffered engine failure and crashed near Great Massingham, in Norfolk.

16

P-51D-15 44-15717 *WILD WILL* of Maj Niven Cranfill, 368th FS/359th FG, East Wretham, March 1945

When Maj Niven Cranfill took off from East Wretham on 19 March 1945, he had four aerial victories to his credit, three of which had been scored on a single mission. South of Dessaun Cranfill helplessly watched as ten Me 262s attacked a formation of B-17s. After shooting a jet off a P-51's tail, Cranfill bounced another Me 262, firing several bursts from 800 down to 600 yards and getting good hits. The jet rolled into a diving left turn and went straight in. Cranfill received credit for one Me 262 damaged and one destroyed, making him an ace.

17

P-51D 44-63621 *LITTLE SHRIMP* of Maj Robert Foy, 363rd FS/357th FG, Leiston, March 1945

On 19 March 1945 the 363rd FS was escorting B-17s to targets in the Ruhland. Near Giessen, Maj Robert W Foy spotted three Me 262s bouncing a flight of Mustangs. He went in pursuit of one of the aircraft, but it quickly began to accelerate out of range. Using his K-14 gunsight to good effect, Foy fired a long range burst that set the left engine on fire and the jet rolled over and crashed near an airfield. Foy officially finished the war a triple ace with 15 victories, and one of the two aircraft he was credited with damaging was an Me 262.

18

P-51D (sub-type and serial number unknown) *BUNNIE* of 1Lt Roscoe Brown, 100th FS/332nd FG, Ramitelli, Italy, March 1945

On 24 March 1945, the Tuskegee Airmen of the 332nd FG flew their longest mission of the war – a 1600-mile round trip to Berlin, where they encountered a force of 25 Me 262s. During a ten-minute dogfight 1Lt Roscoe C Brown shot down a jet fighter from 10./JG 7. During the fight two other Tuskegee Airmen scored confirmed victories, with a third claiming a probable. Brown never 'made ace', but he certainly made the most of his one encounter with an Me 262.

19

P-47M-1 44-21160 *"Devastatin Deb"* of Maj George Bostwick and Capt John Fahringer, 63rd FS/56th FG, Boxted, March/April 1945

The P-47M was the fastest piston-engined fighter of World War 2, Republic building just 133 examples – dubbed 'Sprint' Thunderbolts and fitted with the Pratt & Whitney R-2800-57 engine rated at 2800 hp with water injection at 32,500 ft – in an attempt to give USAAF pilots a chance of catching the Me 262. The 56th FG received the first of 108 examples of the ultimate Thunderbolt on 3 January 1945. Although the M-model proved mechanically challenging in service, 44-21160 showed its effectiveness by shooting down two Me 262s. The first was claimed on 25 March 1945 when Maj George E Bostwick 'made ace' when he shot down a jet that was attempting to land at Parchim airfield. On 5 April, an Me 262 pilot made the fatal mistake of getting into a turning fight with Capt John C Fahringer, who quickly despatched the jet, forcing the pilot to bail out. This was Fahringer's fourth, and final, victory of the war.

20

P-51D-20 44-63668 *LIVE BAIT* of Capt Clayton Gross, 355th FS/354th FG, Y64 Ober Olm, Germany, April 1945

On 14 April 1945, five-victory ace Capt Clayton K Gross spotted a single Me 262 near Alt Lönnewitz airfield and split-essed into a full throttle dive from 12,000 ft in pursuit of the aeroplane. He was nearly killed when his Mustang was gripped by compressibility as he exceeded 450 mph, but Gross managed to pull out 'on the deck'. His overtaking speed was so great that he only managed to fire a quick, albeit well-aimed, burst before overshooting. His fire blew the jet's left wingtip off, forcing its pilot – probably Gefreiter Kurt Lobgesang of 1./JG 7 – to bail out. This was the sixth and final victory for Capt Gross. His aircraft, 44-63668, was subsequently passed on to the 338th FS/55th FG and then transferred to the 308th FS/31st FG, before being sold to the Swiss Air Force as J-2087. It was eventually acquired by the Nicaraguan Air Force in the 1950s and written off there.

21

P-51D-20 44-64147 *BIG DICK* of Capt Richard Hewitt, 82nd FS/78th FG, Duxford, April 1945

In the final weeks of the war there was seemingly no slacking in Luftwaffe jet operations, and on 17 April Capt Richard Hewitt and his wingman, multiple jet killer 1Lt Allen Rosenblum, chased a pair of Me 262s to an airfield in Prague, where Hewitt shot down one of the fighters on short finals for his fifth victory. However, Rosenblum was shot down over the same field and became a PoW, and as there was no clear gun camera film from Hewitt's Mustang, his ace-making victory was listed as unofficial and remains so to this day. Post-war, 44-64147 was transferred to the Italian Air Force.

22

P-47D-28 42-28453 *The Irish Shillalah* of 1Lt James Finnegan, 10th FS/50th FG, Y90 Giebelstadt, Germany, April 1945

On 25 April 1945 American and French B-26s were heading into southern Germany, escorted by P-47s, when they were subjected to a devastating attacked by five Me 262s from JV 44 that were being led by unit CO, Generalleutnant Adolf Galland. As he attacked the Marauders, Galland's fighter was hit by a burst of defensive fire from TSgt Henry Dietz, a waist gunner on board Capt Gunther Gurkin's B-26 from the 34th BS/17th BG. From above, 1Lt James E Finnegan saw the jets and immediately pursued Galland's ailing Me 262, firing two well aimed bursts that finished the fighter off. Depite being wounded, Galland managed to belly land his jet back at Munich-Riem airfield.

23

Tempest V JN817/JF-H of Flt Lt A E Umbers, No 3 Sqn, B80 Volkel, Holland, 21 October 1944

New Zealander Flt Lt Arthur 'Spike' Umbers had achieved several victories flying the Typhoon IB with No 486 Sqn in 1942-43, and after joining Tempest V-equipped No 3 Sqn in 1944 he became a

V1 ace. After moving with the unit to the Continent, he made one of the first jet claims by a Tempest V pilot when, at the controls of this aircraft, he damaged an Me 262 near Nijmegen on 21 October 1944. Unlike Umbers, who was shot down and killed by flak while leading No 486 Sqn as its CO during an attack on Meppen airfield on 14 February 1945, JN817 survived the war.

24

Tempest V EJ750/JBW of Wg Cdr J B Wray, No 122 Wing, B80 Volkel, Holland, November-December 1944

As was the privilege of his rank, Wg Cdr John Wray, Wing Leader of No 122 Wing, had his assigned Tempest V marked up with his initials. He was flying this aircraft on 3 November 1944 when he damaged an Me 262 over the German-Dutch border near Geldern to register his first aerial combat claim. Wray was flying it again when, on 5 December, he destroyed an Me 262 of I./KG(J) 51 for his sole confirmed aerial victory. On Christmas Day he attacked an Ar 234 that was credited to him merely as damaged when, in fact, it subsequently crash-landed and was wrecked. EJ570 was itself written off in February 1945 when its pilot was forced to crash-land after being hit by flak. The fighter had by then been passed on to No 486 Sqn.

25

Spitfire IX MK686/DB-L of Flt Lt J J Boyle, No 411 Sqn RCAF, B88 Heesch, Holland, 25 December 1944

Flying this aircraft soon after midday on Christmas Day 1944, 22-year-old Flt Lt John Boyle received the ultimate Christmas present when, over his base at Heesch as he returned from a sortie, he sighted an Me 262. He had encountered a jet two days earlier, but had only managed to damage it. On this occasion, however, Boyle set the machine on fire and Oberleutnant Hans-Georg Lamle of I./KG(J) 51 subsequently crashed to his death. This aircraft was the second of Boyle's six victories. MK686 was later transferred to the French *Armée de l'Air*.

26

Tempest V EJ523/SA-D of Plt Off J D Bremner, No 486 Sqn RNZAF, B80 Volkel, 25 December 1944

New Zealand V1 ace Plt Off Duff Bremner achieved his first aircraft victory when, near Aachen on Christmas Day 1944 in concert with Flg Off Jack Stafford, he shot down an Me 262. Bremner attacked the jet after Stafford, and following his second burst he watched the pilot bail out. Duff Bremner remained with No 486 Sqn into 1945. EJ523 did not survive the war as it was wrecked in a crash-landing on 25 February 1945.

27

Spitfire IX PV213/AH-W of Capt K D H Bolstad, No 332 (Norwegian) Sqn, B79 Woensdrecht, Holland, 14 January 1945

Having joined No 332 Sqn as a second lieutenant in 1943, Capt Kåre Bolstad had been promoted to command 'B' Flight by

January 1945. During a sweep in company with fellow Norwegian-manned No 331 Sqn on 14 January 1945, Spitfires from both units became engaged with the fighter cover near Rheine airfield. At least five Me 262s were also seen, and diving down, Bolstad claimed his second victory when he destroyed one of the jets. He was promoted to command his squadron soon afterwards but on 3 April he was shot down by flak and killed whilst strafing (in PT834) near Zwolle, in Holland. PV213 had also been destroyed by then, the Spitfire being lost to unknown causes during a sweep on 16 February.

28
Spitfire IX ML141/YO-E of Flg Off D W Church, No 401 Sqn RCAF, B88 Heesch, Holland, 23 January 1945

On 23 January 1945, Flg Off Don Church was on a sweep in ML141/YO-E when he spotted Ar 234s of III./KG 76 taking off from Bramsche. Diving in after the Arado bombers, Church succeeded in sending one crashing to its destruction for his fifth, and final, claim, three of which were for aircraft destroyed. In a very successful action, other pilots shot down two more Ar 234s and damaged three more, whilst five were damaged on the ground. Church survived the war but ML141 fell victim to light flak whilst strafing a train near Hamburg on 25 April, its pilot bailing out.

29
Mosquito VI TA386/ZQ-F of Flg Off R E Lelong, Fighter Experimental Flight, Wittering, 22 March 1945

The Fighter Experimental Flight formed part of the Central Fighter Establishment's Night Fighter Development Wing, which was tasked with developing night intruder tactics and procedures. The Flight was manned by experienced crews, one of whom was New Zealander Flg Off Roy Lelong and his navigator Plt Off J McLaren, who by early 1945 had achieved seven victories. Using Coltishall as a forward base, the Flight flew intruder missions over German airfields and took a steady toll of aircraft on the ground – including three Me 262s that Lelong hit at Neuburg on 22 March 1945. Lelong remained in the RAF postwar, although TA386 survived only a matter of weeks after VE Day. The Mosquito was damaged beyond repair when it swung on takeoff and lost its undercarriage in an accident at Y9 Dijon on 19 June 1945.

30
Mustang III KH503/NK-Z of Flt Lt K C M Giddings, No 118 Sqn, Bentwaters, 23 March 1945

Flt Lt Mike Giddings, who had earlier become an ace flying Spitfires (with Nos 249 and 118 Sqns in 1942 and 1944, respectively), made his only claim with the Mustang III during a long range bomber escort for a raid on Bremen on 23 March 1945. When the 100 Lancasters came under attack from around 20 Me 262s, Giddings attempted to intercept the jets but they proved too fast for a decisive engagement. Nevertheless, he claimed in his Combat Report that he saw strikes

which had inflicted structural damage on the starboard wing of his target. Giddings remained in the RAF post-war and rose to the rank of Air Marshal, whilst KH503 also survived the conflict, to be scrapped in 1947.

31
Mustang III FB385/WC-W of Flt Sgt A Murkowski, No 309 (Polish) Sqn, Andrews Field, 9 April 1945

On 21 February 1945 Flt Sgt Toni Murkowski claimed No 309 Sqn's first aerial victory when he shot down an Fw 190D-9 25 miles east of Utrecht, in Holland. A few weeks later, on 9 April, he was part of an escort to Hamburg that engaged a group of Me 262s, and he claimed one of four jet fighters that were shot down – the final Polish victories of the war. He also damaged a second jet. Murkowski joined the RAF post-war and served until 1975, whilst FB385 was struck off charge in 1947.

32
Spitfire XIV SM826/EB-B of Sqn Ldr J B Shepherd, No 41 Sqn, B106 Twente, Holland, 14 April 1945

Sqn Ldr John Shepherd was flying this aircraft on a sweep north of Bremen on 14 April when, near the airfield at Nordholz, he spotted a Bf 110 that was towing an Me 163. He attacked and was credited with both aircraft destroyed. These were the first of his eight victories in the Griffon-engined Spitfire. His mount, SM826, was itself an 'ace' aircraft that had flown in several other successful actions. Unlike Shepherd, who perished in a flying accident in Germany on 22 January 1946, SM826 saw extensive post-war service until becoming an instructional airframe in December 1948.

33
Spitfire XVI TD147/JF-E of Wg Cdr J F Edwards, No 127 Wing, B154 Soltau, Germany, 29 April 1945

During the last days of the war in Europe, Wg Cdr 'Eddie' Edwards, who was one of the leading Canadian aces of the conflict, returned to action as the Wing Leader of No 127 Wing. On one of his first sorties (on 29 April) when flying TD147, which was marked as his personal aircraft, he had two combats and succeeded in damaging an Me 262 – his only claim against a jet. The next day he opened fire on another Me 262, but it climbed away and escaped. Edwards had a full career in the post-war RCAF and eventually became a group captain, whilst TD147 was transferred to the Royal Hellenic Air Force in 1949.

INDEX

Note: locators in **bold** refer to illustrations and captions.

aircraft, British: Mosquito **29** (**43**, 95), **84**; Mustang III **30** (**43**, 95), **31** (**44**, 95); Spitfire IX **25** (**42**, 94), **27** (**42**, 94–95), **28** (**43**, 95), 74–75, 76, 77–78, 79; Spitfire XIV **32** (**44**, 95); Spitfire XVI **33** (**44**, 95), 78; Tempest V **23** (**41**, 94), **24** (**41**, 94), **26** (**42**, 94), 74–75, 76, 78, 80, 81, 84
aircraft, German: Ar 234; 6, 12–13, 28, 33, 52–53, 71; He 162; 6, 14–16, 86; He 280; 9–10; Me 163; 6, 7–9, 17–23, 29–30, 54, 79–80, 84; Me 262; 6, 9, 10–12, 13, 23, 24–29, 30–32, 45–51, 54–56, 57–59, 60–61, 63–70, 71–73, 74–83, 85–87; Storch 6–7
aircraft, Russian: La-7; **13** (**38**, 92–93), 88–89; Yak-3; 89, 90
aircraft, US: B-17 Flying Fortress 17–18, 20–22, 31, 46, 66; B-24 Liberator 29, 58; P-38 Lightning 18–20, **1** (**34**, 91); P-47 Thunderbolt 23, 24–25, **2** (**34**, 91), **4** (**35**, 91), **19** (**40**, 93–94), **22** (**41**, 94), 59, 63; P-51 Mustang 13, 27–30, 31–32, **3** (**34**, 91), **5** (**35**, 91), **6** (**35**, 91–92), **7** (**36**, 92); **8** (**36**, 92); **9** (**36**, 92), **10** (**37**, 92), **11** (**37**, 92), **12** (**37**, 92), **14** (**38**, 93), **15** (**38**, 93), **16** (**39**, 93), **17** (**39**, 93), **18** (**39**, 93), **20** (**40**, 94), **21** (**40**, 94), 45–46, 49
Allen, Capt Merle 31–32
Amoss, 2Lt Dudley 'Dixie' **12** (37, 92), 48–49
Anderson, 1Lt Robert H 26
Andreas, Lt Günter 29
Arnold, Hptm Heinz 26
Audet, Flt Lt Dick 80–81

Bär, ObLt Heinz 15, 73
Barnhart, 1Lt Robert E 53–54
Bätcher, Maj Hansgeorg 51
Beaudrault, Capt Valmore J 24–25, **2** (**34**, 91)
Bley, ObLt Paul 27, 28
Blickenstaff, Maj Wayne K 49, 50
Blume, Walther 12
Bochkay, Capt Donald H **11** (**37**, 92), 47, 69, 70
Bollenrath, Obfw Jakob 29–30
Bolstad, Capt Kåare **27** (**42**, 94–95), 79, **80**
Bostwick, Maj George E **19** (**40**, 93–94), 59, **60**, **61**
Boyle, Flt Lt Jack **25** (**42**, 94), 77–78
Bremner, Plt Off Duff **26** (**42**, 94), 78, **79**
British Army 16, 57
Brown, 1Lt Roscoe **18** (**39**, 93), 57, **58**
Browning, Capt James W **10** (**37**, 92), **45**, 47–48
Bryan, Capt Donald **14** (**38**, 93), 52–53
Buttmann, Hptm Hans-Christoph 75, **76**

Campbell, Flg Off Frank 74
Candelaria, 1Lt Richard G 64–65
Cannon, 1Lt Joe 56
Carson, Maj Kit 69
Carter, 1Lt Johnnie L 47, **48**
Ceuleers, Lt Col George F 62–63
Church, Flg Off Don **28** (**43**, 95), 80
Cole, Plt Off Bob 72
Coleman, 1Lt Wayne 23, 61
Collier, Sqn Ldr Jim 78
Compton, Capt Gordon B 49–50, 66
Conner, Maj Richard E 26
Cox, Flt Lt Neill 85–86
Cranfill, Maj Niven K **16** (**39**, 93), 54–55, **56**
Crosthwait, 2Lt Edwin M, Jnr 59
Cummings, Capt Donald M 50–51

Daniel, Col William A 57–58
Delatowski, Uffz Edmund 75
Dietz, TSgt Henry **71**, 72
Doolittle, Lt Gen 'Jimmy' 28
Drew, 1Lt Urban 'Ben' 27–28, **3** (**34**, 91)

Edwards, Wg Cdr James 'Eddie' **33** (**44**, 95), 87

Fahringer, Capt John C **19** (**40**, 94), 63
Fiebelkorn, 1Lt Ernest C 'Feeb' **31**, 32, **7** (**36**, 92)
Fifield, Capt Robert S 55–56
Finnegan, 1Lt James J **22** (**41**, 94), 72–73
Foy, Maj Robert W **17** (**39**, 93), 47, **48**, 55, 56, **57**
Fraser, Flg Off Hugh 81

Galland, GenLt Adolf 10, 11, 25–26, 32, 51, 72–73
Garland, Flt Lt John 'Judy' 76–77
Gaze, Flt Lt Tony 82, 85, 86
Giddings, Flt Lt Mike **30** (**43**, 95), 83
Giller, Maj Edward B 65
Glover, Capt Freddie **28**, 29, 30, **5** (**35**, 91)
Göring, Hermann 8, 11, 14, 52
Götz, ObLt Horst 13
Gross, Capt Clayton K **20** (**40**, 94), 67

Harbison, Flt Lt Paddy 82–83
Haslope, Flg Off John 'Slops' 84, **85**
Haydon, 1Lt Edward 31–32, 46
Hayes, Lt Col Tommy 55–56
Heinkel, Ernst 9–10
Hewitt, Capt Richard **21** (**40**, 94), **67**, 68
Hitler, Adolf 10, 11, 32, 51
Hooker, Capt Verne E 64

Jeffrey, Capt Arthur F 18–20, **1** (**34**, 91)
Jones, 2Lt Cyril W 21–23

Karger, 1Lt Dale K **9** (**36**, 92), 46
Keller, Adolf 48
Kirchner, Fw Günther 15–16
Kirk, 1Lt John A 56
Kobert, Lt Gerhard 27
Kozhedub, Maj Ivan **13** (**38**, 92–93), 88–89
Külp, ObLt Franz 57
Kuznetsov, Snr Lt Ivan 90

Lamb, 2Lt Huie H 28, 29, **4** (**35**, 91)
Landers, Lt Col John D 60–61
Lange, Uffz Kurt 89
Lauer, Obfw Hieronymous 23, 24–25
Lippisch, Alexander Martin 6–7
Littge, Capt Raymond H 58–59
Lobgesang, Gefr Kurt 67
Luftwaffe: JG 1; 15, 16; JG 7; 32, 45, 49, 60, 63, 66, 90; JG 400; 8–9, 20, 30; JV 44; 51, 71–73, 90; KG 76; 52; KG(J) 54; 46–47, 50, 51

McCandliss, 2Lt Bob 27, 28
McCoppin, 2Lt Bill 27, 28
MacKay, Flg Lt John 75, 79, 86
MacLeod, Flt Lt Frank 80
Manrer, Wilhelm 48
Merkvaladze, Snr Lt Garri 90
Messerschmitt, Wilhelm 'Willy' 7, 10–11, 14
Meyer, Fw Hans 78
Meyer, Lt Col John C **32**, 33, **8** (**36**, 92)
Milch, Erhard 8, 10, 11
Mullins, 1Lt Reese Walker 20
Murkowski, Flt Sgt Toni **31** (**44**, 95), 83
Murphy, Lt Col John B 20–21, 22
Murray, Flt Lt Frederick 80
Mussells, Sqn Ldr Campbell 83–84
Myers, Maj Joseph 23

Norley, Capt Louis 'Red Dog' 29–30, **6** (**35**, 91–92)
Nowotny, Maj Walter 26, 31–32

Olejnik, Hptm Herbert 8
Olmsted, Merle 48
operations: *Bodenplatte* (1945) 45, 79; *Clarion* (1945) 49; *Market Garden* (1944) 74; *Overlord* (1944) 12–13; *Varsity* (1945) 56–57

Penn, Capt Donald E 50
Philo, Capt Herbert A 73
Pöhs, Josef 8

Rake, Flt Lt Derek 85
Rebeski, Hans 12
Rechenbach, Lt Hans 16, 87
Red Army Air Force (VVS KA) 15, 88–90
Reid, Flt Lt Danny 84
Ridley, 1Lt Oscar 69–70
Riedesel, ObLt Volprecht Freiherr von 48
RLM (Ministry of Aviation) 7, 10, 12
Rosenblum, 1Lt Allen A 26, 28–29, **67**, 68
Royal Air Force (RAF) 74–87
Russel, Obfhr Heinz 27, 49
Ryan, Maj Eugene E 68
Ryll, Lt Hartmut 20, 22

Sampson, Sqn Ldr Ralph 'Sammy' 78
Saur, Karl Otto 14
Savitskii, Lt Gen Yevgenii 89
Schäfer, Fritz 9
Schall, Lt Franz 26, 89
Schallmoser, Uffz Eduard 72
Schmitt, Lt Rudolf 16
Schnörrer, Lt Karl 48, 60
Schreiber, Lt Alfred 11
Schuck, ObLt Walter 66
Seager, Flt Lt Tony 75–76
Sedvert, 1Lt Theodore W 51
Selle, FlgKap Heinz 12
Shafer, Lt Col Dale 70
Shepherd, Sqn Ldr John **32** (**44**, 95), 85
Shoffit, 1Lt Jimmy C 22
Shouse, Flt Off Russel E 54
Simpson, 1Lt Richard G 20
Sivko, Lt L I 89
Smith, Flg Off Keith 86–87
Smith, Sqn Ldr Ron 75
Sommer, Lt Erich 13
Späte, Maj Wolfgang 8
Speer, Albert 11, 14
Stafford, Flt Lt Jack 78
Straznicky, Fw Herbert 20, 22, 30

Tacon, Col Avelin 17–18
Teeter, 1Lt Robert 24–25
Thain, 2Lt Thomas V 60, 61
Thompson, 2Lt Hilton O 63–64, 70–71
Titarenko, Maj Dmitrii 88–89
Tordoff, 1Lt Harrison B 61

Udet, Ernst 7, 9
US Army Air Force (USAAF) 15; Eighth 26, 58, 60; Fifteenth 57; Ninth 24–25, 33; 4th FG 29–30; 20th FG 66; 50th FG 72–73; 55th FG **49**; 78th FG 23, 60; 332nd FG (Tuskegee Airmen) 57; 339th FG 13; 352nd FG 32–33, 66; 353rd FG 49, 66; 354th FG 66–67; 357th FG 30, 45–48, 55, 68–69; 359th FG 17–18; 364th FG 31, 51, 62–63; 479th FG 18, 63–64

Varley, Flt Lt George 84–85
Vorozheikin, Maj Arsenii 90

Walkington, Flg Off Geoff 15, 16, 86
Weaver, Capt Charles E **68**, 69–70
Weber, Lt Joachim 11
Welter, ObLt Kurt 16
Wenk, Friedrich 6
Wetmore, Capt Ray S **15** (**38**, 93), 54, **55**
White, 1Lt Richard E 51
Winks, 1Lt Robert P 45–46
Wollenweber, ObLt Wolfgang 16
Wray, Wg Cdr John **24** (**41**, 94), 74–75, 76, 77

Yeager, Capt 'Chuck' **24**, 30–31
Yeardley, Flg Off Albert 82, 83